THE THRESHOLD OF PARADISE

PARADISE

A NOVEL

BY

JOSHUA COLLINS

The Threshold of Paradise
Copyright © 2011 by Joshua Collins

Library of Congress Control Number: 2011928795
Collins, Joshua, 1980-
The Threshold of Paradise
ISBN 978-1-935434-59-7

Subject Codes and Description:
1. FIC027020 Fiction: Romance - Contemporary
2. REL006080 Religion: Biblical Criticism and
Interpretation - General 3. LAN005540 Language
Arts and Discipline: Composition and Creative
Writing - Genre Fiction

Cover art by Barton Green

Published by
FACT•ION
an imprint of
GlobalEdAdvance PRESS

gea-books.com

ACKNOWLEDGEMENTS

May posterity smile on the names of the

precious individuals recorded here.

May they know that they are cherished eternally.

This book was commissioned by Dr. Leonard Heller and his wife Elizabeth Heller. The Hellers served as extremely generous patrons for the composition of the manuscript. Furthermore, they supplied whatever books I needed for my research, and they left the books with me as gifts. As patrons, they affected the manuscript's contents in no way other than by editing it for misprints; they merely wished to see the end of my research presented publically as I saw fit. I hope this product is found by them to be satisfactory.

Rev. Donna Kasik, with a rare kindness, gave me full use of her property, literature, and resources in order to construct this manuscript as I deemed appropriate. She invested in this work financially, she purchased a multitude of research materials for me, and she also availed herself as an editor for misprints. Without Rev. Kasik, the manuscript could not have been completed in the time-frame in which it was finished.

Miss Sharon Rehanek served as an editor for every draft of this manuscript. She offered helpful suggestions, critical insights, and creative reflections that served to polish the final draft. Sharon's literary eye was beyond beneficial, and she personally contributed a sizable amount of literature as an aid to my research. Without Miss Rehanek, this manuscript would have had rough edges due to various, unavoidable constraints.

Sharon, Rev. Kasik, and the Hellers have my affectionate gratitude for their respective contributions, for their undaunted aid, for their delicate concern, for their continual care, and for their stellar character. Enough cannot be said concerning the selflessness and generosity with which they showered me. Had it not been for the steadfast faith of these beautiful people, my manuscript may never have become the book before you. I have been given beyond what I can repay.

"HIS COUNSELS TREAD THE MAZE
OF LABYRINTHINE WAYS
THROUGH QUICKS, THROUGH GLOOMS WITH UMBRAGE
OVERGROWN..."

(From *The Suppliant Maidens,* by Aeschylus)

CHAPTER 1

The first chapter is like the last, and the makings of a circuit have begun. What begins as a small garden will become a....

□□□

The bright, spring, Saturday morning was crisp, dewy, and cloudless. Sunlight filled the royal blue sky and resplendence spilled through an open window into the little living-room of Jim and Sarah on their first wedding anniversary. Jim stood before the bathroom mirror as he shaved off the bristles that surrounded his smile. Sarah stood in the living-room and leaned through her third-story window as she occupied herself with her hanging flowerbox.

Jim emerged from the bathroom in his plush, blue robe and worn, earthy slippers. Sarah stood with her back to him as she busied herself with the contents of the flowerbox that she had removed from its hanging position outside of the windowsill. Sarah's soft humming tickled Jim's ears. Jim's aftershave exuded a fresh, regal scent that caught Sarah's attention, and she turned with an illustrious, widening smile towards her husband as she

continued to hold the wooden flowerbox. Jim grinned in return and approached his young wife. The two stood silently with only the flowerbox in Sarah's slender hands between them. Jim leaned over the wooden box, peered into Sarah's eyes, and gave her an affectionate, little peck upon her forehead. Sarah looked up at Jim with a radiance that had been growing since he had first slipped her wedding ring on her finger. She raised the flowerbox a couple of inches and asked, "What do you think?"
Jim closed his eyes and sniffed Spring's scents which wafted from the vivid petals that crowned Sarah's box; "…smells wonderful, Sarah."

"Open your eyes, Silly," said Sarah playfully. Jim opened his eyes and found them locked in his wife's gentle gaze. His smile was large, his hopes had no limit, and his joy was replete. Everything seemed so full… so overflowingly full. His wife was the apex of beauty to him. Her voice dripped with sweetness to him. Jim was entirely captivated by the woman he had married one year before. "Jimmy," said Sarah, "I meant for you to look *inside* the flowerbox."

"Oh… I'm sorry. Hey! Wait a minute; are those the figurines from our wedding cake?" asked Jim, with a mixture of curiosity and amusement. The dimensions of the little figures caused the stems of the flowers to appear as mighty trunks in comparison. The plastic couple seemed to stand peacefully in a garden where the tree tops were giant, perfumed petals.

Sarah beamed. "Yes. What do you think?"

Taken aback, Jim answered, "What a neat idea! — putting them in a hanging flowerbox.... Wow! That's really creative, Sarah."

"I thought you'd like it. I thought it would be fitting for our first anniversary."

"It is," answered Jim. "It's like they're in their own, little world... some kind of love-domain, or paradise, or something. I don't know... like something from some ancient time." His wife smiled. Jim gazed at his lovely spouse with a tenderness that he could only feel and not fully explain. "It reminds me of how I feel about you."

"What do you mean, Jim?"

"I mean, when I stand next to you, I feel like a king! It's like no one else even exists except for the two of us." Jim's eyes grew softer and gentler. Sarah's eyes grew wider and more receptive. The two young lovers shared some resounding, yet unspoken, language that was only perceptible in their respective hearts, and it seemed to them as if they could read each other's silent speech impeccably. "You're more beautiful than all of these flowers, and I don't deserve to be standing next to you; but here I am..."

"Oh, Jim," Sarah blushed; "you're embarrassing me."

"…only because you can't accept the truth."

Sarah smiled. "I love you too, Jimmy," she said, with an almost school-girlish manner.

Jim's chest seemed to inflate.   "You can't possibly love me as much as I love you."

"Stop it."

"No, no; I'm serious. There's no way that you can possibly love me as much as I love you," he asserted.

"That's just not true," she replied as she blinked at him with eyelashes that resembled happily flapped feathers.

"How do you figure that?" asked Jim playfully.

"Remember, *I'm* the one who put us in this little garden; *I'm* the one who made a little paradise for Wedding Cake Jim and Sarah. So there!" said Sarah with an air of playful defiance, as she spun on her heels like a bird amusing itself in mid-air, enraptured by the sheer joy of being able to fly.

"Oh yeah?"

"Yeah!" she contended. Jim descended upon his pretend prey —"Ouch!" squeaked Sarah in reaction to the little pinch that Jim was giving her. Jim took flight like a little child through their tiny apartment, with his lovely wife running after him, giggling all the way.

CHAPTER 2

A year-and-a-half later.

Sarah loved Fridays, since Friday was what she and Jim called their "Date-night"; they would eat out at, or order food from, one restaurant or another, together and undisturbed. Sarah returned home from work in cheery expectation of her husband. Jim had suddenly begun working a significant amount of overtime during the past week, and the young couple had experienced a lack of togetherness. Since it was Friday, Sarah anticipated a brief break from the week's drudgery and a little indulgence in a good meal coupled with carefree romance that disregarded clocks. Sarah hurried to the bathroom where she began to freshen up for her beloved, who would be arriving home from work at any moment.

As she stood before the bathroom sink, just as lovely and sweet-smelling as she was that very morning before work, she heard her front door unlock, open, and shut. Her heart fluttered. Sarah hurried out from before the sink to greet her work-weary husband. She entered the living-room and found Jim slumped upon their dilapidated sofa as he stared into space and drummed his fingers on the fraying armrest. Sarah stood before him in a pose that rivaled a classical statue.

"Hi, Honey," said Sarah with a buoyant smoothness. Jim took a quick, careless glance at his adorable wife, and then returned to his blank stare into nothingness.

"Hi," he quietly muttered in cold, aloof response to Sarah's warm, inviting greeting. Jim then arose and walked into the kitchen where he opened the refrigerator door and began browsing indifferently. Having inadvertently furrowed her brow, Sarah strutted after her husband.

"Are you tired? You've had a hard week, haven't you?" asked Sarah as she approached Jim from behind and embraced him delicately. Jim behaved with disinterest and removed himself from before the refrigerator and his wife.

"What's the matter, Jim? Aren't you glad to see me?" she questioned as she beamed with adoration. Jim finally returned a smile, though his smile was but an imitation; his eyes concealed his truest feelings from Sarah with a blank and blinkless fixedness.

"Hi, Honey,' said Jim in a monotone manner. "I'm eating out with Brian tonight."

"Oh... uhh.... Why? I mean... yeah, ok; no problem," Sarah stammered with wounded confusion regarding her husband's unexpected abruptness and atypical breach of their "Date-night."

"I'll see you later. Don't wait up," said Jim unexcitedly, as he exited the kitchen.
Sarah stood in the kitchen, alone and bewildered. She found Jim's reaction strange compared to his usual fondness for her entwined with his habitual Friday giddiness. Sarah could hear that Jim busied himself on one side of the wall while she stood with stupefied inertia on other side.

"I love you, Jim," said Sarah in a voice that was loud enough to reach his ears in the living-room before he left their tiny apartment. "I said, I love you, Jim," repeated Sarah, as her speech was interrupted by the sound of the front door closing.

A nauseating churning began to overturn her stomach. Hot and cold waves produced tiny beads of sweat near her hairline that moved the condensation down her face. A cold, pressing sensation pushed its way from her collar-bone up towards her chin along either side of her neck. Sarah ran into the bathroom, knelt, and succumbed to an unexpected and vehement sickness that ended as quickly as it had begun.

CHAPTER 3

Sarah awoke the next morning to a still darkness. She considered how pleasant it was to awake before the dreaded blast of her sadistic alarm clock that she nick-named "The Bomb." Before she switched the nightstand lamp on, she turned over towards her husband's side of the bed to give him a good-morning hug; however, after reaching sleepily with her arm, she found that her husband was not on his side of the bed, nor in any other part of it. Confusedly, Sarah sat up, and as her eyes began to focus in the morning obscurity, she saw that she had arisen nearly 15 minutes later than she usually did before work; then she realized that it was Saturday. She subsequently wondered why Jim had awoken before sunrise on what was usually a sleepy Saturday morning. "Jim?" she called out, not knowing what was going on. "Jim?"

"What?" she heard Jim respond, in an annoyed and garbled manner, from behind the partially opened bathroom door as he brushed his teeth.

"Oh... I was just wondering what was going on," said Sarah in a yawning, drawn-out, drowsy manner. "Why didn't you wake me up?" Jim did not respond.

Shaking the sleep from her dizzy head, Sarah sat up, plopped her feet onto the creaky floor beside their bed, and arose with the stiffness of morning's slow-motion. As she drew near the bathroom, Jim departed from it towards the kitchen. "Good morning."

"Hey," he said flatly, as he continued uninterruptedly towards the kitchen, past his patiently awaiting wife. Sarah was still standing with her eyes closed and her cheek exposed before she realized that Jim was not standing next to her ready to give her the usual good-morning-peck. Sarah tore her sleep-sewn eyes open, and with a somewhat mystified expression, sauntered groggily towards the washroom. After having brushed her teeth, she followed Jim, who sat in their small kitchen at their rickety table, where he ate rather hurriedly and sat somewhat hunched over with tired eyes.

"Did you two have a nice meal last night?" asked Sarah as she poured herself a cup of steamy, nutty-smelling coffee.

"Oh, right... last night.... I didn't meet up with Brian after all." Caught off guard, Sarah quizzically raised her head and kindly asked,

"Uh... well, then what *did* you do?"

"I went for a long walk; then I just got some fast food," said Jim as he avoided making eye-contact with Sarah. Jim ate with a rushed disinterest as he cleaned his plate with the careless clanging of his silverware.

"But you were gone for hours."

"Yeah, Sarah; I know. I just needed some time to think. Brian wasn't home and I couldn't reach him."

"So you hadn't planned this thing before you told me what you were going to do last night?" Sarah asked in a somewhat injured manner.

"Look, I'm tired. I had a long day yesterday, ok?"

"Long day? You got home right after I did, Honey."

"I meant a *hard* day. I had a hard day yesterday; it just felt long."

"Do you want to talk about it? Is everything ok?"

"Everything's fine," said Jim, with an edge of contracting patience. I just needed some time to myself... to unwind. I just, kinda, hit the wall yesterday, and I needed to relax."

"We could have relaxed together..." said Sarah smilingly, as she reached across the little kitchen table to caress her husband's hand; however, he pretended not to notice, withdrew, arose from his seat, and placed his dishes in the sink.

"I gotta get to work," said Jim, as he left the kitchen.

"On Saturday?"

"Yeah; overtime...." Sarah sat with her coffee in her hand; she remained cool while her coffee steamed. Sarah arose to follow her husband. As Jim slung his coat over one arm, Sarah attempted to hug her husband who received her embrace reluctantly; he offered only a paltry, nonchalant pat with his left hand on her back.

"I love you, Jim."

"See-ya later." The door opened for less than a second and shut for more than ten hours.

CHAPTER 4

A week-and-a-half later.

The tension between the two young lovers had become unbearable for Sarah. Jim had hardly been home for more than a half-hour before he went to sleep each night, even though his overtime work-day ended two hours before his normal bedtime; since he only worked 20 minutes away from home, the numbers did not seem to compute to Sarah. When questioned concerning his whereabouts, Jim would grow defensively angry, and he only answered with an obtuse deflection that side-slipped the issue. In a short time, a wide disconnect had torn the couple's communication into shreds of half-answered questions and acute shards of misapprehended statements. An unseen yet suffocating weight bore down upon the home of Jim and Sarah. "Suspicion" could be painted, with substantial endurance, on the invisible wall that had been erected between the once elated love-birds who occasionally flew into the unseen pane.

Jim's eyes had always appeared to Sarah as transparent passageways to his inner feelings, and she often understood her husband's ponderings prior to his usually open articulation of them. Throughout her two-and-a-half years of marriage to Jim, Sarah had always had confidence that she possessed the key to Jim's heart; however, the recent degeneration of communication that had cropped up between the two had concealed Jim's feelings with a highly-brandished lock while Sarah stood seemingly helpless with but a cracked, glass key. Sarah's otherwise sweet manner had been melted into a frustrated, reactive sharpness that extended from the wounds of Jim's occasionally whetted tongue.

"What did you say?"

"You heard me!"

"Don't you talk to me that way!" yelled Sarah.

"This is *my* house, and *you* are not going to tell *me* what to say, or anything else; back off!" demanded Jim angrily.

"*Your* house (!)?"

"Yeah, that's right, Sarah; '*my*' house!"

"Stop it! You're talking like a nut! Calm down"

"— You calm down! You're yelling!"

"*You're* yelling! You've been ignoring me for over a week now. I want to know what's the matter. You don't eat dinner with me. I don't know where you go after work, I —"

"— I told you, I've been working late."

"Every night?"

"Yeah, every night! You said you'd like that house down the street, right (?); so I'm working late every night so that we can get it."

"Then why are you so angry with me all the time? I didn't do anything to you."

"Leave me alone, Sarah! I'm tired! I'm annoyed! The last thing I need from you is to give me even more stress...."

"What do you mean, 'Leave me alone,' Jim? I'm just trying to figure out what's the matter, that's all."

"Nothing's the matter. Look, I'm going to be late for work; I gotta go."

"When will you be coming home?"

"I don't know...late. I'm working late, alright?"

"I'll call you tonight after I get home, ok?" asked Sarah.

"Whatever. I gotta go. See-ya." The key broke off within the lock.

□□□

"Hello?"

"Um... yeah, hi. Is Jim Davis there?"

"Jim Davis? No. He left over an hour ago. Can I take a message?"

"Uh, yes... well, no, I guess not. That's ok. Thank you."

□□□

The evening sun had only recently set, and Sarah already lay in her bedroom in wait of sleep — but, more so, she waited for her husband's return. Small streams of bluish light crept through the slits of the blinds that hung over their bedroom window. Sarah lay in silence... in sadness... in the conflict of churning stillness. Blue hues of thinning light deepened into dim shades and purplish rays that blended together and caused shadows to flee away into the ensuing oblivion that follows a fading day's departure. The night was still and quiet. Sarah felt an uneasiness that led to a disquieting unrest. She lay on her bed, and the sheets felt cold and empty. She lay with open eyes that were cast upon the place where her husband was supposed to be lying. The shadows of the room continued to decline until they reached that point where darkness begins to grow, at a seeping pace, so as to envelope the last stand of resilience offered by the diminishing gleam of the once stalwart sun. The final flicker of Sarah's pulsing ponderings sunk into the sands of solitary sleep.

□□□

"Jim?"

"Go back to sleep; it's late."

"What time is it?"

"Good night, Sarah."

CHAPTER 5

A week later.

Sarah flushed. She had, yet again, been overcome by sudden nausea. The rapid onset of momentary sickness had become more frequent as of late. After washing her face and brushing her teeth, Sarah trudged into the living-room, sank into the couch, and sat in silence with sadness. She and Jim had hardly spoken more than a paragraph to each other for several days. Sarah had eaten dinner alone for over two weeks, and the weight of each somber night closed her lids in the solitary confinement of lonesome dreams. She sat and stared at the wall, despite the open book on her lap. She couldn't concentrate. Sarah closed her book, stood up, and began to tidy the little apartment. After having made a circuitous and meaningless route of quasi-cleaning, she flopped back down on the old sofa in a manner half-way between sitting and lying. She was agitatedly depressed… restless, yet drained of energy from her strangely frequent and unpredictable stomach bouts. Sarah's eyes widened. She launched from the couch, threw her coat on, grabbed her keys, and headed for the store.

□□□

The home-pregnancy-test was positive; Sarah realized that she was an expectant mother. A whirlwind of emotion began to swirl cyclonically in her mind. She exhaled hot gusts as she considered her recently cold encounters with her husband. Her eyes clouded with dismal density until the rain broke out onto her cheeks. The young mother sat under the storm's lashing, alone.

☐☐☐

Sarah picked up the phone and dialed.

"Hello?" said Sarah's best friend on the other end, as she attempted to remove a sliver from her finger.

"Hi, Tina."

"Hey, Sarah; what's going on?" asked Tina, as she fumbled with the telephone.

"Oh nothing; it's just that... well...." Almost immediately, Sarah began to lose her composure; "I... wish... I... think," sniffled Sarah; "I just want him back... I just want back the man I married... It's like I don't know who he is anymore..." and Sarah's flood gates opened upon her friend with an unexpected surge that began to drain both of them. Sarah wept with all the bitterness of an impending winter that did not hint at any more springs.

"What do you mean that you don't 'know him any more?' What's happened? How long has this been going on?" asked Tina with sincere concern for her best friend.

"I'm just so tired of the constant fighting... the constant loneliness... the waiting, the hoping, the..." she could not finish her sentence except with a deluge of gulping attempts at steady breath that gave Tina the impression of a lone swimmer drowning in salty despair.

"Please, calm down; just tell me what's going on," urged Tina compassionately.

"We just keep fighting, Tina — that is, when we actually talk. It seems like every other night we get into something that ruins the next day. We go to sleep angry. We just aren't what we used to be. He used to hold me. He used to tell me how beautiful he thought I was. He used to do things with me and go places with me. Now, I barely even see him, and when I do, we just fight. I want back the husband I married... I don't want what I have now. Why can't it just all stay the same? Why can't...." Sarah broke into a shattered state that reflected silver hopes scratched by a marred reality.

"What did you two fight about this time?" asked Tina.

CHAPTER 6

The next morning:

Jim rushed to and fro about the tiny apartment while readying himself for work with reddened, sleep-stung eyes. Sarah followed him, as she put her earrings on, and she questioned Jim as to why he had not returned home until long after she had fallen asleep. "Who's out 'till 1:30 on a Monday night, Jim? It's not like you were at work that late or something. Where were you?"
"I don't have time for this, Sarah!"

"Jim, wait…"

"I'm going to be late for work!"

"Then just be late, once! We gotta work this out, Jim."

"Look, I'll be home around 10 tonight; I'm working late. We'll talk then."

"You're always working late!" He ignored her. "Jim? Jim!"

"Enough!"

"No! I'm sick of you just leaving all the time without finishing anything! I can't stand this! You're going to talk to me, now! What's going on? Why are you being like this (!)?"

"I can't take your nagging, and I —"

"— Nagging (!)?"

Jim turned away from Sarah with a disgusted expression, lowered his voice, and said coldly, "I'll see you some time."

"What's that supposed to mean? Huh?" Jim opened the front door and walked through it. "Wait!" said Sarah, as the front door closed in front of her. "Wait," she whispered to the closed door.

CHAPTER 7

Two days later.

The evening air was chilly and vaporous. It appeared as though the clouds hung just above the concrete, and both seemed to be the same dismal color. Smoldering scents sifted through the sun-setting sky as the ghosts of burning leaves rose to meet their brothers in the clouds. A slight mist sprayed through the air and hybridized with the smoky perfume yielded by various leaf-piles upon being consumed in the burn-pits of backyard fires. Autumn's strange immingling of opposites augmented Sarah's mixed emotions; she felt as if the enflamed glory of the decaying foliage was a natural similitude to the interleaved paradoxes of life.

Sarah perceived that her marriage was becoming enmeshed in folly, and she began to wonder if it had been consummated in like. Her starry-eyed lashes had once fluttered for her beloved Jim, but presently her horizon had grown dim before Sorrow's shady wing. Sugar-coated syllables once glided from lip to ear between Sarah and Jim, but the cool exchanges of late pointed towards the indifferent dusk of oblivion.

The chill of the intermittent wind-pulses penetrated Sarah's jacket and occasionally tugged on her umbrella. The consistent frigidity of her unraveling connection to Jim tugged the cords of her heart. Autumn's wetness infused rigid decay into all that was once supple and sublime; the slow, yet unrelenting, pattern of the Reaper's season began to dominate with time on its side. Bright yellows melted into tempered golds. Sanguine crimsons congealed into deep shades of rust. One manner of tint was exchanged for another, and the autumnal watercolors were painted brightly upon a drab, dewy curtain that curtailed the resplendence of the sun. A growing sullenness began to pervade the air that had once rung with the sounds of songbirds. The mellifluous words that once wafted between Jim and Sarah had soured.

Sarah rang Tina's buzzer. "Who is it?" Tina's voice projected from the intercom.

"It's me, Sarah." Sarah heard the electronic click that unlocked the front door to Tina's apartment building; she opened the outside door, ascended three flights of stairs, and went to Tina's apartment where she was met by her smiling friend. Sarah looked weary.

Seeing the remnant of Sarah's strength begin to diminish, Tina enclosed Sarah with a cheerful hug. "Come on in; let's talk about it." The two friends entered the small, dilapidated apartment and rested on Tina's sofa that threatened to collapse each time anyone dared to sit on it.

After a few uncomfortable, quiet minutes elapsed, Sarah sighed and said, "I just wish I could get him to talk to me... he never has time any more. You know, I think about my grampa and the way he used to talk.... It's like... I don't know... in his day, it seems like people graduated from high school, the man got a job, the woman stayed home, and people just built a life together. Then I think about today; we need three degrees to get a dime-a-dozen job, and we get married late because of it; both the husband and the wife work... both have two separate careers that seem to go in two different directions... we come home, eat, and try to make something out of an hour per night.... What kind of relationship is that? How does that really work? *Does* that really work?" Tina frowned as she listened. "I was always told that if you love someone enough, things just find a way of working themselves out. I try to keep a positive attitude, but I'm finding that a lot of my attitudes aren't realistic. It's like we're taught to make our lives resemble fairy-tales, but we often forget what fairy-tales are."

"What do you mean?"

"I mean, we try to make our realities resemble fantasy, but reality is reality and fantasy is fantasy."

"I think the goal is to get our lives to be as close to the fairy-tale as possible."

"I don't know, Tina. If that's true, why haven't I met anyone who lives out the princess story? Why do the knights in shining armor always seem, eventually, to fight against the damsels instead of fighting for them like they once did?"

CHAPTER 8

The next evening:

Sarah returned from work to her little apartment. She opened the door and walked into an empty silence she had begun to know all too well. She could feel the quietude. She could feel changes taking place inside her body.

Sarah walked over to the living-room window and stood in front of the moist sill; she liked to leave at least one window slightly open in the autumn because she enjoyed the crisp, damp scent of the season. The aroma of people burning leaves blended with the cool, pluvious air and produced a sublime paradox of opposing elemental essences. Sarah opened the window even wider so that she could look into her miniature hanging garden.

She had first formed the world of Wedding Cake Jim and Sarah in the springtime. The soft verdure of the spring season that surrounded the figurines was once crowned with iridescent petals that had aromatized her recollections of bliss with a savor that could nearly turn back the scythe of time for her by a simple sniff. Only a year-and-a-half ago, each inhalation of her miniature flower-world's luxuriant scents would inadvertently remind her of her first kiss as the wife of Jim Davis. However, the autumnal day at hand produced different results.

The seasons had changed guard, and her miniature garden had become bitten by chilly winds and cold rains. Inside the box stood the little bride and groom figurines beneath withered vegetation. Sarah had, at first, scolded herself for not taking her little garden inside on account of Autumn's algid breezes. However, as her situation with Jim became dimmer, she had become more defiant in defense of her makeshift world, her dreams, her memories... and she left the little garden to brave the real elements in fictional fortitude as she attempted to brave the storms that had arisen between her real husband and herself.

When she had planted her fantasy, the world of Wedding-cake Jim and Sarah had been lush and optimistic; it had grown towards the light; it had flourished through the direction of gentle hands by which well-crafted care cultivated increasing grandeur daily. However, as Summer's vigor yielded its authority to Autumn's sap-draining strength, cold showers had begun to efface the upturned crescents where unalloyed enchantment was once cast. Sarah took special notice of the eroding smiles on Wedding Cake Jim and Sarah. She felt her body changing.

The dewy, rainy gusts of the fall season had diminished the felicitous expressions of the figurines in a manner similar to how an overabundance of tears can vaporize what was once confidence in veracity. Sarah continued to gaze at the dematerializing grins of the figurines, the wilting garden, the declining light of a sunset concealed within clouds that were pregnant with rain... an unlined canopy devoid of visible silver that served as a graying back-drop for a weathered love.... She turned away from the model world that once was and beheld her crumbling existence that was present and real. Nothing in her flowerbox garden resembled what it was supposed to represent, and both of her worlds were slipping into the coolness of undesired change.

CHAPTER 9

The next evening:

Blazing colors continued to flare at the behest of the Autumn's dreary tears that raised the season's lament as high as the clouds. Sarah drummed her fingers on the armrest of her couch. After sitting in silence for a while, she rose and readied herself for repose. Sometimes, she felt that sleep was the only anesthetic for loneliness; strangely enough, as loneliness can be difficult to escape, so can sleep be difficult to obtain.

Sarah lay on her bed and watched what remained of the sunlight mingle with darkness in the last dance of the dying day. She wondered why quietude can be deafening sometimes. She wondered why the multicolored splotches that painted the autumnal landscape were so designed to display their glory only at the onset of the season of death; it was as if all of nature sung a swansong... an exclamation whose truest vigor can only be brought about by impending doom. Darkness crept into Sarah's bedroom with its usual silence, and it sought to usher her into the disturbed slumber of another raw, rainy, fall night — alone. Sarah lay on her side

and watched the clock tick towards the making of
unmemorable dreams.

☐☐☐

She awoke to the sightless sound of her tip-
toeing husband moving about in the living-room. As
he lay down on the squeaky living-room couch, Sarah
called out, "Jim?"
"Yeah?"
"What's going on? Come in here," she yawned.
"Go back to sleep; I'll see you in the morning."
"Jim?" It was silent. "Jim?"

☐☐☐

Friday:

"Thanks for breakfast, Sarah," said Jim thinly
and from the living-room, as he thrust his arms
through the sleeves of his overcoat.
"I'm glad you liked it," Sarah said while she
washed the morning dishes and leaned tiredly against
the wall that separated the living-room from the
kitchen. After a short pause that seemed no longer
than eternity, Sarah asked, "Do you think that we can
talk this evening? I hate having problems hang over
our heads... I just love you so much, and I want us to
be happy..." She heard no response. "Jim?"

Sarah turned the faucet off, dried her hands with the rag that hung on the refrigerator door. She stepped into the empty living-room that Jim had recently left on his way to work.

"Jim?"

CHAPTER 10

One Week Later:

Though the recent weeks had been nothing short of arduous, Sarah had planned an evening with her husband in advance. Since her attempts at conversation with Jim in their home had fizzled into futility, her design for this particular "Date-night" was to set a mutually appreciated stage upon which to enter, slowly, into a discussion of her pregnancy, of which Jim knew nothing. Sarah was surprised and relieved that Jim even agreed to celebrate another weekly "Date-night" in light of his retreat and self-encasement into unexplained disaffection.

Two consecutive Date-nights had been missed due to Jim's supposed "over-time," and one was altogether obliterated by an irate discussion that blew the remainder of the evening to the floor of a teary ocean. Sarah noticed that her words also had become tainted by an irritated tone, and her less than stellar reactions to the undisclosed source of her husband's agitation served to occult her very attempts at throwing light upon their present gloom. Sarah regretted the fact that she had begun to mirror her husband's frustrated negativity, and so she had orchestrated this particular Date-night as an active attempt to wipe away the obscuring difficulties that reflected darkly upon both her and her beloved. Sarah felt her stomach begin to rock like a small, open boat upon a churning sea.

□□□

Jim and Sarah stood, in their bedroom, next to their mirrored closet. Sarah was adorned in a lovely evening dress. Jim shuffled around in the process of changing out of his regular work clothes. He began to button his fresh shirt.

"What do you mean I 'work too much'; how else can I afford that house you want?" said Jim, with obvious irritation.

"I'm just saying that you're never home for dinner anymore, we never have any time together anymore, I can't ever get a hold of you while you're working late, and I'm just getting tired of it, Baby; that's all." Sarah stopped for a second, drew in breath, and tried to ignore the cramping that was taking place in her abdomen. "Let's just relax."

"Look, Sarah, I don't know what you're up to while I'm gone at night and working my tail off.... I'm tired, I'm frustrated, and I'm at the end of my rope. After 65-hour weeks, the last thing I need to hear is you complaining about me," he responded with physical weariness as he stripped his khaki pants and redressed himself in black suit slacks.

The pit of Sarah's stomach pressed within her, and in an attempt to control her tone, she replied, "What *I'm* 'up to?' Wait.... First of all, I'm not complaining about *you*, I'm just tired of the situation. "I'm not 'up to' anything but waiting for you to come home at night."

"Look, I *am* home, and I *was* planning on a really nice evening tonight too, ok?" Jim shoe-horned himself into his freshly polished wingtips. "Then, you have to open your mouth and start screwing things up by complaining and nagging and whining...." said Jim, as he walked into the kitchen with his dirty laundry in his hands. He tossed his shirt and pants into the washing machine, and his pants clanged against the inner walls of the machine on account of the keys that were accidentally left in one of the pockets.

"...stop it, Jim! I'm not complaining about *you*," said Sarah, as she began to lose control of her tone and as nausea began to cause her voice to tremble. "I just asked you where you've been all of these evenings and I want to know when life is going to be normal for us again."
Jim slipped into his suit jacket. "You act like *I'm* doing something wrong! I told you over and over and over that I have to work late for a while. That's

it! That's all there is to it! Stop calling my job to ask when I'm coming home; I'll be home when work is over!"

"Jim!" shouted Sarah, as she lost control of herself.

"Enough! I'm sick of you asking me the same question over and over…. I'm worn out, and you're making it worse!"

"I'm not trying to make it worse; I'm trying to have a fruitful marriage!"

"Me too! — but I can't have a marriage with you always on my back every single day! At least you know what *I'm* doing every night," said Jim.

"What's that supposed to mean?"

"I'm at work every night; that doesn't mean that you're at home every night, does it?"

"What are you implying?"

"Why are giving me that guilty look, Sarah?"

"What guilty look? — what are you talking about(!)? I thought we were talking about your ridiculous work schedule!"

"I'm just saying that you call me at work, and there I am; but, I call you from work, and I usually talk to the voicemail."

"What? First of all, you haven't been there several times when I've called you 'at work.' Besides, do I have to sit here by the phone and just wait for you to call or come home? Can't I see friends? Can't I go out?"

"I can't account for your whereabouts."

"What are you saying? You can call Tina's whenever you want to; that's where I usually go anyway."

"I have, several times; I got her answering machine each time."

"Well, we don't always just sit in her house. Sometimes we go out for coffee or to a show or something."

"How convenient."

"Hey! This house gets pretty quiet night after night when you're gone. Sometimes, I just want to get out, since waiting for you is, obviously, not paying off!"

"Not paying off? I'm doing this *for* you!"

"Are you?"

"I'm sick of this, and I'm getting sick of you right now. Stop complaining! Stop whining! Stop calling!"

"Stop yelling! Stop demanding!"

"I finally get an evening off, and you ruin everything! I'm done! I don't care what day it is!" shouted Jim as he headed for the front door.

"*Wait!*" screeched Sarah, as she reached for her husband in an attempt to prevent him from leaving. She clung to his arm with her slender hands as hard as she could, but Jim shrugged her off of him and pushed his way through the front door. "Jim!" shouted Sarah, but he ignored his wife and continued to walk out into the poorly-lit stair-hall. Jim descended the apartment-building's staircase, opened the front door, and the dimming, gray sky's blurry condensation enveloped him in nebulosity.

Sarah stood alone in her apartment. Her abdomen continued to cramp. She began to double over as she ran towards the bathroom in tears.

CHAPTER 11

Jim descended the concrete steps of the porch before the front door and walked across the building's parking lot with his chin down and his hands stuffed inside of his pockets in an attempt to keep warm. Upon reaching his car, Jim felt around for his keys; however, he found no keys in his pockets, and he realized that he must have forgotten them in their apartment. He turned back towards the apartment building. He took one step forward. He stopped, as he was not yet prepared to return home to his wife so soon after their recent discord. He pulled out his phone from his jacket-pocket and struck a note on the key-pad.

"Hello?"

"Hey, Brian."

"Jimmy-boy! What's happening?"

"Oh... nothing; hey, are you free tonight? Wanna meet up?"

"On a Friday? Isn't Friday your... Yeah; sure pal; we can meet up."

"What's all that noise in the background?"

"I'm at Malik's Sports-bar & Grill... the

finest place in town for down-and-out single men like myself," Brian remarked with sarcastic self-abasement; "Why don't you just meet me here."

"Sound's ok to me; I'll be there in about 20 minutes."

"Alrighty. Hey Lisa, can I have another..." (click); Brian hung up.

Jim stuffed both of his hands back into his pants' pockets, ducked his head in reaction to the wet, windy chill, and began a brisk walk to Malik's. He passed by their apartment-building's front door; he paused again, as he was tempted by the uncomfortable temperature to retrieve his keys. He thought of Sarah. Angrily, Jim's expression grew cross as his eyebrows sank into a fixed stubbornness, and he defiantly turned away from the door and headed for Malik's to see his best friend.

CHAPTER 12

Jim's penetrating words had cut Sarah beyond an evening's repair. However, she faulted herself as well for failing to exact the subtle method she had intended to guide her plan for reconciliation. Despite the near worthlessness of their conversation, Sarah had discovered that Jim was reacting to something... that his present iciness was more the defensive isolation that accompanies a wound than it was the dissipation of romantic drive. It seemed to her that Jim was accusing her of something that he could not bring himself to utter.

Through her tears, Sarah reflected upon the last month and the strange, straining events that had severed the sublime relationship she had so enjoyed with Jim. Jim's behavior had turned with the abruptness that typifies a light-switch. The sombrous reality that stood before her appeared to have something to do with some offense that Jim had taken from her and with which he was, apparently, unable to cope.

Sarah's eyes burned as they were being uncontrollably washed with sadness. She tried to take her mind off of things by straightening up her small apartment; it did not work. She opened the newspaper; it did not help. She went over to the washing machine and turned it on. She turned her back to the machine and leaned on it for support. The sounds from the noisy washing machine helped drown out her sobbing. Slowly, Sarah slumped down upon the kitchen floor, with her back against the machine. She moved her feet closer to her body so that her knees stood as tall as her shoulders. As she leaned her elbows over her knees, Sarah wept in the loneliness of what she perceived as a personal defeat.

 "Why doesn't he love me any more?" she whispered to herself.

CHAPTER 13

"Hi, Brian."

"Hey-ya Jimmy," said Brian loudly. Brian's cold bottle dripped with condensation as Jim sat down across from him in the booth next to a dusty window in a dim corner of the sports-bar; "...just enjoying a cool one... know what I mean?"

"Jim... Wzup?" asked the owner, who leaned to one side while he sat on a stool and puffed his favorite cigar. "What's new? Can I get you something?"

"Yeah: a cold one, and some cheese-sticks," responded Jim.

"You got it," answered the owner in his deep, rusty voice. "Lisa, get Jim a cold one and some cheese sticks," the sports-bar owner ordered his sultry, smiling employee, who silently assented to his raspy direction with a half-nod.

Jim sat opposite Brian in Brian's favorite booth. Jim peered through the dusty window at the dreary day before him. The clouds seemed to hang with a weighted curvature that bowed towards the earth with a quiet oppressiveness. The heavens began to weep upon the ground. His eyes blinked rapidly in an effort to conceal the condensation that yearned to water his cheeks where only a superficial smile grew. His glance was darkened by rows of tired wrinkles that folded below his eyes and above his efforts to hide a string of sleepless nights; the manifestations of Jim's weariness gave the impression of upturned rows of soil upon which anguish had been planted and about which thorns grew. Jim continued to peer through the dusty window.

"Jim!" blurted Brian, as he broke Jim from momentarily locked despondence.

"Yeah, Brian?"

"You come over to my table while I'm watching some of the greatest sports clips of all time, you sit down right below the T.V., stare out the window for ten minutes, and leave poor Lisa standing here with your drink and cheese-sticks without even saying hello to her," barked Brian facetiously.

"Sorry, Lisa," said Jim with only partial seriousness, though he was shocked that time had elapsed so quickly without his notice. He felt semi-exposed.

"Don't worry about it, tiger," Lisa responded with a liberal air of overreaching familiarity. With a curling smile that mingled interest with feigned concern, she silkily asked, "What's the matter, hun?"

"Nothing, Lisa. I've just had a long week, and I get a little worn out by the time Friday rolls around."

"I get off at 10 o'clock tonight, if you want to talk about it," said Lisa, as she curled a glistening lock of her long, lustrous hair with her slender index finger. Brian raised an eyebrow, but then returned to the T.V.

"We'll see," said Jim. With clammy hands, he clutched his shiny bottle, raised the neck to his lips, and took a quick, careless taste of the sweaty drink. The diamond on Jim's wedding ring flashed brilliantly in the subtle lights of the sports-bar and projected a flicker of unspoken disenchantment across the countenance of the young, attractive waitress. She laid a gentle hand on Jim's shoulder, turned, and strutted away in her usual, colorful manner while Jim did his best to keep his eyes to himself so as not to support the eyebrow Brian had raised again. After an awkward silence between Brian and Jim, Brian turned again to watch the highlights. The crowd on the T.V. roared.

"Whoah! Did you see how he slammed on that guy? I could watch that clip every day," Brian exclaimed in reaction to the television. Having noticed that Jim paid neither the T.V. nor his company any attention, Brian finally asked, "Jim, what's the deal?"

Jim's forehead was moist. His eyes were nearly ready to burst; using the heat of the situation as an excuse, Jim took his bottle, touched it to his forehead, and slyly moved it over his eyes as he leaned forward and bowed his head in order to cool himself with his drink so as to have an excuse to wipe his face, and eyes, with his napkin. "It sure is hot today," said Jim. Brian raised another eye-brow; "Hot? It's 45 degrees outside." Jim turned his abashed glance outside and beheld the browning verdure of Fall's colorful, deathly touch.

CHAPTER 14

Thirty minutes passed. Sarah's tears began to dry from the exhaustion that so often accompanies heavy crying. The washing machine had stopped, and Sarah's little apartment felt like a giant void. All was quiet and motionless. Sarah stared into space. Her knees began to stiffen from having sat for 30 minutes on the floor, and so she erected herself. She did not know what to do or where to go, so she began transferring the clothes from the washing machine into the dryer.

Only seconds after having turned the dryer on, a loud clanging rung from inside the machine. Sarah opened the dryer door and the machine automatically shut off. Once again, Jim had left something in one of his pockets and had subsequently thrown both the garment and the article within it into the laundry. Sarah poked around the soggy clothes within the dryer until she felt a hard mass in a pair of Jim's pants. Having pulled the pants from the machine, Sarah dug her hands within a pocket and drew out Jim's keys, along with the soggy shreds of a note. Sarah's eyes scanned the remains of the dampened, paper message before her, and she felt an utter devastation pierce her belly.

▢▢▢

"Hello?"

"Hi, Tina," sniffled Sarah.

"What's wrong? Are you sick? You sound like you have the sniffles," asked Tina from the other end of the phone.

Having paused momentarily, Sarah attempted to muster some fragment of composure, but she then deluged her attempt at discourse with unwanted anguish: "I found a note in Jim's pants pocket... you know how he's always leaving things in his pockets.... We got into another fight, and he left the house... you know.... I tried to take my mind off of things, so I tidied up a little... I tried to sit and read the paper... I couldn't concentrate...."

"Newspaper ink and tears mixed together make for a pretty muddy read," said Tina, as she failed in her corny attempt to elicit a chuckle from her sorrowful friend.

"I got up and went over to the laundry closet to run a load. When I turned the dryer on, I heard Jim's keys banging around inside the machine; you know how he's always forgetting to empty his pockets?" she repeated.

"Yeah, yeah, uh-huh —"

"— so, I opened the machine, pulled out the pair of pants with the keys still in them, and I found shreds of a note in the same pocket."

"So, what did it say?" asked Tina.

"I could only read a little of it because the rest fell apart when I pulled it out, and even the part that I could read was really smeared." Sarah sniffled a couple of times, but then she erupted with distress, "...it was written by a woman... and... the... only parts... she was really... she really wants him..." Sarah sobbed without restraint. Tina's mouth hung open, and her eyes bulged.

"Your husband is cheating on you?" asked Tina. "He is cheating on you (!)? No! Jim?"

"I... don't know... it seems... I just don't... I can't...."

"Sarah, get a hold of yourself!" Tina's eyes began to blur. "Look, why don't you just come over. We'll get a pizza and figure this whole thing out. Just get out of the house for a little while and cool down. We'll figure things out."

"Ok, Tina; I'll leave now," said Sarah in a defeated manner. The two ladies hung up. Sarah zipped up the overnight bag she had been packing while she talked with Tina. She left the apartment and left the dripping fragment of the note she had found on the counter. She stepped out into the darkening day, opened her umbrella, and ran to her car, splashing all the way.

CHAPTER 15

The cool, damp breeze sifted the variegated leaves with kaleidoscopic patterns that caused multitudinous tints to flutter from tree branches in a spectrum of dying glory. The multicolored foliage was strewn upon the face of the earth in preparation for the transformation to dull decay like many stalwart soldiers who lay about gasping out what remained of their fervor, only to succumb to ashen reality. The raw wind wet the once passionate leaves with the caresses of the increasingly chilly equinox that would eventually sting like the tail of a scorpion.

Sarah stood on the stoop of Tina's apartment building. The awning above the stoop kept her relatively dry. Sarah rang the buzzer to Tina's apartment. Instead of hearing the usual electronic click that unlocked the apartment building's front door, she heard Tina's footsteps swiftly shuffling down three flights of stairs. The door opened, and when Sarah attempted to greet her faithful friend, a flood of weeping unleashed from her gentle eyes and out of what used to be an attempt at a smile-wreathed "Hello." She crumpled before the presence of Tina who, after drawing Sarah from her well of disconsolation, escorted her into the apartment-building with caring shoulder-pats all the way up the stairs.

Upon reaching Tina's tiny apartment, Sarah smelled a warm pizza's scent wafting through the doorway where she slipped off her heels. Tina ushered Sarah into the little abode and invited her to recline on her tattered couch while Tina busied herself with bringing the pizza and soda into the somewhat decrepit living-room.

Tina's small apartment had a hint of antiquity about it. The walls were plaster, and they were cracked in many places. The baseboard was large and much abused by years of careless feet, furniture moving, and the simple degradation that accompanies time like a king accompanied by his executioner. Carpet of an inferior quality covered the majority of an old, hardwood floor that had character etched randomly all over its surface. The apartment appeared to have been, at one time, a compact, yet upscale, abode; but, it had certainly lost its youth. However, Tina's tidiness and cheerfulness dressed the dwelling with sunny hopefulness and jovial comfort that even the wealthiest of snobs would have been compelled to appreciate.

Tina reentered the neat and aging room, placed the warm pizza next to Sarah on the couch, and sat Indian-style in her fuzzy, worn-out pajamas on the thin, coarse carpeting. Tina popped the top of a soda can and handed it to Sarah. The dewy soda can slipped through Sarah's sapped hands. Sarah lunged towards the floor in a vain effort to prevent the spill that had already occurred on the small throw-rug. Tina gave a friendly chuckle and said, "Relax; it's clear pop… it won't stain. I'll clean it up. Just try to calm down. Take off your coat; it's still wet, you know."

"Sorry, Tina," Sarah said.

"Sorry for what? I'll be right back." Sarah slipped her coat off. She was wearing a flowing, elegant evening dress, as if she were ready for a night on the town with her husband. Tina returned and exclaimed, "Whoa! I'm still proud of my little apartment, but you didn't have to dress for the occasion. Where are you going?"

"Jim and I were going to the Grand Hotel's Paradise Restaurant for dinner and then to the Elixir Lounge for dessert."

"Pretty ritzy," Tina remarked, though she had momentarily forgotten that Sarah would not be going to the Paradise Restaurant nor to the Elixir Lounge that evening. Sarah began to sniffle and tear. Tina, having become conscious of her blunder, said, "Oh, I'm sorry Sarah; I'm a dope. I was just trying to compliment you. You always have been so darn pretty. Remember, when we were kids, how jealous I was of you? Hey, do you remember when I tried to curl my hair to look like yours, but then I fried the right side so that, when I combed it, about six inches fell off? Not bad for an eight-year-old, huh?"

"You were 14."

"Who's counting? Come on, have some pizza," said Tina as she nudged the box towards Sarah and proceeded to leave the room in search for cleaning materials. Sarah took a slice as Tina returned to clean up her teary friend's spill. Tina left the room again to dispose of the towel and to wash her hands.

Contemplating the potential liquidation of her marriage, Sarah stared out of the rain-smeared, sliding-glass door that led to Tina's third-story balcony and beheld the liquescent clouds as they appeared to pour from the bottoms of some onto the tops of others. Tina returned to Sarah, who sat with a posture that appeared to hang heavily over the edge of the couch. Tina plopped down on the carpeting, picked up a slice of hot pizza pie from the couch slightly above her and said, "Tell me about it."

CHAPTER 16

Jim slumped backward into the scratched, faux-leather backrest of the dusty booth. His usual practice of feigning stoicism in the face of adversity was beginning to fail before his trusty friend, Brian. Jim appeared to have been inflated and then subsequently pricked with a pin, for his aspect and posture painted a portrait of defeat. Staring into nothingness, in the midst of the steadily increasing clamor of the sports-bar, Jim sneered, "She doesn't love me any more, Brian."

"What do you mean, 'She doesn't love you any more,'?"

"Just what I said, she doesn't love me any more. I've worked long hours just so that I would be able to save more money for the down-payment on that house she's always wanted, you know, the one on 2nd Street... night after night after night at my boring job pushing papers for my pushy boss, all so that I can give her that stupid house — "

"— and she doesn't love you for all of that work! What's with that? I have no patience for that kind of stuff. You know, I once worked overtime for a while just so that I could buy a girl a nice dress and take her out to eat at a fancy restaurant."

"What happened?" asked Jim.

"She went to the prom with Bill Stevenson," said Brian bitterly.

"That was ten years ago, Brian."

"Who's counting? Look, the point is that I know what it's like to work your brains out for nothing when you've got your mind on some dame."

"You 'worked' overtime at the convenience store while you thumbed through magazines, ate candy-bars, and watched sports on T.V. — when you were 18-years-old. How does this compare to my marriage now?"

Brian shouted to the owner of the sports-bar, "Get Jim another cold one! He's not being cooperative, nor is he being sympathetic to my former sorrows." Jim gave a sort of chuckle as he took a swig. Brian blinked slowly at Jim. The owner left Lisa in charge, pulled a drag from his cigar, and departed momentarily through a cloud of sweet-smelling smoke.

"Seriously, Brian —"

"— I was just trying to make you laugh, Jim; I heard you… you gave me a chuckle-huff."

Jim grinned; "A what?" Then the two of them began laughing, and Brian's laughter was sincere.

Jim began again, "I've worked so hard for this house —"

"— well, has she been pushing you for this house?"

"No, I guess not."

"Then what's the problem?"

"I don't know...."

Lisa, the waitress, brought another cold, sweaty bottle over to Jim and handed it to him instead of placing it before him on the table; she then strutted away; Brian kept his eyes on Jim. "I just wonder if I married Sarah for the right reasons. I mean, she was only 22. There's a big world out there, and I feel like I kind of boxed myself into a corner of existence that doesn't pay for extra effort."

"Well, buddy, what more do you want out of life? You have a decent job, your car runs, you eat every day, and you're married to a smart, pretty girl."

"So what? There has to be more to life than those things; lots of people have those things. Besides, Sarah is getting a little pudgy in the middle"; at that, Brian appeared to be stabbed by some invisible knife held by some unseen hand that produced visible results before Jim's eyes as he watched his friend lean back in his seat with a barely audible but highly visible exhalation. In his focus on himself, Jim forgot....

"Look, Jim. You know that my unit got called up only two months after I married Jenny; remember? I was gone for two years... I was away from my new wife — who I was only married to for two months —

when I had to go fight in that desert. I didn't want
to do all kinds of things, but I had no choice. I came
back with all kinds of hopes for Jenny and me... I
couldn't wait for our first embrace in two years... I
found out that she was pregnant a month later; I was
so happy I could bust! — until I found out I wasn't the
father."

CHAPTER 17

Tina's soothing resilience had always been one of her most outstanding traits. When others were sunk in melancholy, Tina spoke and acted so as to uplift them... and when she herself was gripped by grief, she restrained herself amazingly in an attempt not to burden others. She was a rarity regarding faithfulness, and her intrepid joviality was a good fit for anyone fortunate enough to have her as a friend. Sarah, nearly swallowed by her grievous situation, began to explain her circumstances.

"Jim and I have been fighting so much lately."

"About what?" asked Tina.

"Everything."

"How often?"

"All the time."

"Well we can't talk about 'everything,' and we can't do it 'all' at once. Why don't you pick a spot you want me to hear, and I'll listen," said Tina with a sunny smile. "Have some more pizza."

Sarah leaned back in her seat. Her evening dress sparkled with an glossy shimmer as the golden threads that were delicately woven into the black fabric glinted under the small ceiling light that hung over the tattered couch. Her hair shined like the dark, tear-stained shadows below her eyes. She gazed into the despair of her thoughts as she looked fixedly upon the ceiling.

"Sarah?"

"Huh? Oh, yeah, Tina; I'm sorry. I'm just wiped out."

"Tell me about it; what's been going on with you and Jim?"

Sarah sat up, leaned forward, and buried her face in her hands. "Jim has been 'working late' a lot lately. At first, I was really impressed with his work-ethic... but, after a while, it seemed as if Jim wasn't interested in me personally, for some reason. I don't know... maybe he just, sort of, lost that spark for me or something."

"You haven't been married very long."

"Well, the romantic stuff has died down an awful lot; it just seems to keep dwindling. I mean, it's not like it was when we were first married. It's like, no matter what I do, Jim's just not absolutely crazy about me anymore; lately, it's been a million times worse. Maybe I'm just not attractive to him anymore; I don't know."

"That's crazy! You were always the prettiest girl in the bunch, the prettiest girl on the block, the prettiest girl in school... c'mon, Sarah; get real."

"...but he used to remind me of how attractive he found me, and he used to shower me with compliments. He used to praise my cooking, the way I kept our apartment... everything. Both of us work full-time jobs, and since I'm the one who takes care of the house, he would always tell me how nice it was 'to come home to a clean house, a good meal, and a beautiful wife.'"

"So what happened?"

"I don't know. He's been cold; he doesn't answer questions; he won't talk about anything; he's been acting like a nut...."

"...just all of a sudden?"

"Sort of.... He hasn't been *totally* nuts about me for about a year, but at least we got along. We always got along... but, now, it's like he can't stand me."

"Can't stand you? What do you mean? Where's this coming from?"

"It all came on suddenly. It seems that, out of nowhere, we started having little grumbles with each other here and there for a couple of days, but nothing serious. The little grumbles turned into arguments, but we would make up that same evening... well, verbally anyway. Then, within a couple of days, the arguments became more serious, and we would go to bed angry with each other. We started sleeping in different rooms. It was after we started sleeping separately that he began to work even more over-time." Tears streaked Sarah's cheeks.

"I'm sorry, Sarah. I just hate to see you hurt…" said Tina with warm eyes and a hopeful smile. "…how about some more pizza?" Sarah's expression grew from grim to thankful.

"Ok; thanks, Tina." Sarah hungrily grabbed another slice and choked back a mouthful of sobs.

"Nothin' like a big mouthful of food to take away depression!" remarked Tina.

"Shut up," said Sarah, as she chuckled with a tinge of embarrassment.

"It's good, isn't it? …Papa Pizzano's deep dish!" exclaimed Tina in a tone that suggested some blithe remembrance. "Now, that should bring a smile to anyone's face. It's not the Paradise Restaurant, but it sure makes me think of paradise," Tina quipped. "Eat up; the night is young."

Tina's phone rang. Sarah knew it was Tina's new boyfriend who was calling to find out when he could come over. Sarah reflected nostalgically on the times her chest used to palpitate when the phone rang… the times when Jim used to pursue her. Tina, in her usually sweet way, apologized to the young man for breaking their date, but she discretely explained that her friend, Sarah, was dealing with a significant load, and she asked to reschedule the date for the following evening. After a kind telephone departure melded with a promising look into something only Tina could see, Tina told her new boyfriend that she was anxious to see him (the next day), and it appeared that he had responded in congruence.

"Thanks, Tina," said Sarah.

"You have some pizza sauce on your face."

CHAPTER 18

The lights in the sports-bar were dim, and they added to Lisa's attractiveness. She wore a hair-gloss that caused her locks to sparkle in the darkness like the glitz of a lit city skyline severing the shadows of dusk. Her eyes had a flashing quality about them. It was becoming increasingly noticeable that Lisa paid Jim close attention, and she continued to find reasons for being near him beyond the duties of her occupation. Despite the increasing crowd, Lisa always seemed to let her perfume linger close enough to Jim so as to manufacture an almost ever-present aura of distraction for him.

"I'm thinking about calling it quits with her... I've been thinking about it for about a month now," said Jim (as he tried to keep his eyes off of Lisa). "I mean, I love Sarah... or... well, at least I *loved* Sarah..." Jim sighed, though he caught himself before his sigh became a groan. "When I met her, she was so wide-eyed and vibrant — you know, that smile — and she was so happy... she laughed a lot...." Jim began to reminisce inadvertently before Brian, and it was difficult to tell if his eyes were glossy with beatific memories or if they were moist with a sense of seemingly impending disaster. Brian leaned back slowly, took a sip, glanced over at Lisa, who was taking care of other customers, and glanced back at Jim, who, once again, peered through the window that was dusty on one side and soaked on the other. Jim's receding savor of his own recollection was reflected by his somber present. "It just seems like marriage is a mixture of two things that have nothing to do with each other," Jim spoke softly.

"What do you mean?" asked Brian.

"Love and contracts...."

"Ya lost me, pal."

"...remember when we were kids, you know, before we had licenses, how we used to play a lot of ball at the park?"

"Sure, I remember how I used to dominate; yes, I remember that," smiled Brian. The two friends chuckled again. "What are you driving at?"

"What I'm getting at is that we didn't sign any contracts to play ball, and we didn't fill out any paperwork to run up and down with the neighborhood boys; we just played for the love of it. We just enjoyed each other's company for its own sake, which is probably why you and I are still friends, even though you had to go through war ...see what I'm saying?"

"If my ears could 'see,' then yes; but since they don't, I hear what you're saying," grinned Brian.

"I have the Literature degree," Jim retaliated.

"Then you have less of an excuse for your

syntactic misconduct and derelict diction, Jim." The two friends grinned momentarily.

"I mean that if you love someone, shouldn't you just love them for who they are? Shouldn't you just be loved for who you are? It seems like Sarah used to love who I was, but now, it's like she loves me for what I can do, for all of my work, for basically suffering for her so that she can have what she wants."

"Well why do you, or did you, love Sarah?" Jim's expression softened, and his body projected the appearance of an almost immediate relaxation.

"She's such a sweetie; she's really intelligent —"

"— Then why's she with you?"

Locked in recollection and deaf to Brian's kind question, Jim continued, "— she's a good person; she's pretty; she's considerate...."

"Well then what's the problem, Jim? You sit here and rattle off a string of wonderful things about your wife, who you still love, while you contemplate splitting up, and you still haven't explained what in the world playing ball as kids with the neighborhood boys has anything to do with being an adult with a wife."

"Well, I just wonder, sometimes, why love has to be tied to contracts. If you really feel strongly for someone, why is it even necessary to have a contract? Wouldn't you just want to do all that you could for that person, and wouldn't they just want to do all they could for you? If you really love someone, what 'terms' are there to agree upon? It seems that such 'terms' should be met without even trying. When we were kids playing ball outside, in perfect weather or in storms, we just enjoyed the company, the challenge, the camaraderie... so shouldn't it be that, as married adults, through the smooth and the rough, we should just enjoy each other's company, the challenges we face, the companionship we share?" Brian took a swig. "Why does it seem that there are more rough-spots than smooth-sailings? Why are there rough-spots between Sarah and me instead of a situation where the two of us brave storms *together*? I mean, if just being friends with the guys was that much fun, so much fun that you and I are still friends, then shouldn't people of the opposite sex, who are just crazy about each other, who are just crazy enough to get married, be able to be just as in love years later like they were when they first got together? — if that was really the case, we wouldn't need any contracts at all, right? I don't know... I just want to be happy again...."

"Maybe that's what the contract is for, Jim."

"What's the point of it all? — a contract to ensure that arguments won't end and that people won't get on with their lives after their hearts lie to their heads? If love is a feeling, then what happens when that feeling dies?"

"What happens if your premise is incorrect?"

Jim creased his forehead over his headache and replied, "Then your conclusion will be wrong. Why do you ask?"

Lisa wiped down the top of a nearby table. She was dressed rather alluringly for a waitress, and she continued to slip Jim the occasional glance. Thinking that he was undetected by Brian, Jim, occasionally, looked at her with a churning chest of mixed emotions that swirled hurt and attraction, anguish and hope, a trying present and a tempting future, thoughts of Sarah and considerations of Lisa....

"Why do you ask?" Jim repeated.

CHAPTER 19

Sarah and Tina conversed for nearly two hours. The sun sank behind the haze of the autumnal horizon, and the bleak rain-clouds continued to blacken. The dim, yellow light that radiated from Tina's living-room ceiling gave the illusory impression of growing increasingly brighter, though it was the evening sky that was growing steadily darker. Tina's curtains remained drawn, and when Sarah noticed the ceiling-light's reflection in the seemingly obsidian-colored sliding-glass-door, she looked at Tina's plastic wall-clock and remarked with surprise, "I can't believe it's 8:40 already; I've been here for over two hours." The two pieces of pizza that remained in the box were cold. "You didn't have to break your date. I'm sorry I came over on a Friday night. I was so frustrated with Jim that I forgot what day it was, what I was doing, where I was going...."

"...which explains why you were reading a newspaper and doing laundry in a dinner dress ..." Tina giggled. Sarah smirked.

"I've always appreciated you," grinned Sarah; "You can get me to laugh through just about anything."

With a gentle smile, Tina replied, "Don't worry

about me breaking my date. Yeah, I really like that guy, but you're married, and I don't want to see your marriage break apart, but..."

"I don't either, but it seems like Jim has already broken it." Sarah looked up at Tina and gave the bewildered and frightened impression of a child who has just experienced his first punch in the stomach. "How could Jim do this to me?"

"Are you planning on leaving him? Have you thought about it?" questioned Tina.

"I thought you just said that you didn't want to see my marriage break apart."

"I don't; but I don't want to see you in pain either." Sarah furrowed her brow. "Look, I'm just here for you; I just want you to be happy. It comforted me to have my best friend happily married, especially after what happened to my mother just before my dad and her split up. You remember... my mom was just crazy about my dad as far back as I can remember, until she got sick. Since my mom had always been faithful to my dad, it didn't take long for her to put two and two together... and it's a good thing she only got something that was curable with a shot."

Discomfort grew upon Sarah as she listened to her best friend. "I just don't understand how any spouse can botch the whole thing for one night of regret; I mean, no one gets away with it, you know. My mom had every right to leave him."

"Yes, she did," added Sarah indignantly.

"I know she did… but that day is still the saddest day I can remember. I find it almost impossible to overlook the fact that my dad broke our whole family apart because he wanted to have his cake and eat it too. The only way one plus one equals three is by having children," said Tina dejectedly.

"When's the last time you spoke to him?"

"About three years ago; but my mom and I still get together every Sunday. Look, I would never wish a break-up on you, but now-a-days, a shot in the arm might not do much for you if your husband acts like a jerk. I just hate to see you suffer like this; whatever you decide, I'm right behind you, sis."

"Thanks, Tina." Tina smiled warmly at her nearly vanquished friend. Sarah looked around at Tina's cracked apartment nostalgically as she reflected on her own crumbling life. "It sure was a lot of fun when I lived here with you, when we were roommates. We used to eat pizza like this every Friday when we didn't have dates, and we even used to eat pizza with our dates here together too; remember?"

"Of course! It was a blast! Some of my best memories happened over one of these pizza boxes." The two friends smiled together in their reverie. Tina took a sip of her soda, then her eyes widened as she said, "Remember when Jenny and Candice used to come over and we'd have pajama parties? There we

were — 19 and 20 years old having pajama parties...."
Tina and Sarah snickered. Then, slowly, somberness
overshadowed their glee. "Can you believe what
Jenny did to Brian? I *still* can't get over it."

"That was just *awful*. Poor Brian.... I don't
think he's recovered from that," said Sarah.

"I don't think so either. Jenny always was a
pretty shallow person. Sure, she was a lot of fun to
have pizzas and pops with, and she had a ridiculous
sense of humor, but she really was only a good-time
gal, and, looking back, I don't think she was ever
anybody's real friend."

"Yeah, she wasn't very good for her word
either," said Sarah while she remained lost in her
recollection; "but she'd crack us up when we could
actually get her to sit down and stay in one spot
for more than an hour," she added in an attempt
to lighten the present, oppressive load. "I guess we
should have seen it all coming."

"Yeah, I guess you're right. Jenny should have
listened to that bit at your wedding..." and then a
sudden shock slapped Tina into remembrance; "...I
forgot! I keep forgetting!" Tina sprang to her feet and
darted out of the living-room. She returned with a
wrinkled envelope. The envelope was made out with
Tina's address, but with Sarah's name. "I'm sorry,
but I keep forgetting to give this to you. He must have
thought you still live here." Tina handed the envelope
to Sarah. The letter was addressed to "Sarah Peters."

Sarah looked at the return address; the letter was from "Paul." "The guy from your wedding?" asked Tina.

"Yes," Sarah replied with bewilderment. "Yes, he is."

CHAPTER 20

Lisa leaned over a crumb-filled table and wiped it clean with a damp rag. Jim spied her discretely over Brian's shoulder. Brian asked Jim a question to which Jim agreed hastily.

"Yeah, sure; wait a minute. What?" asked Jim.

"I said, if all cats are dogs, and all dogs have two ears, then all cats have two ears; right?"

"Well, wait a second, Brian. Cats have two ears and dogs have two ears; yeah... but that's not true..." Jim stated as he refocused the entirety of his attention back onto his comrade.

"What's not true? — my premise or my conclusion? Surely all normal, healthy cats have two ears, and the same is true for all normal, healthy dogs."

"What you said isn't true in that 'cats are dogs'; cats are cats and dogs are dogs."

"So then which part of my argument is flawed?"

"Your premise; that both cats and dogs have two ears says little to their related natures. A better line of reasoning is —"

"— that even though you feel love, it doesn't mean that love is a feeling? Of course cats are not dogs, Jim; and, of course, love is not a feeling."

"Well, you can't see love, Brian; so, how else could you describe it?"

"Can you see wind?"

"No."

"Well, then by your line of reasoning, how can you account for wind? You're relating feelings to things you can't see, but there are many realities that you can feel and can't see; those realities, in and of themselves, are not feelings. A sailboat isn't moved by feeling, but you can feel what moves the sailboat, and you can see its effects."

"I get your point." Jim took a sip, as did Brian. Jim seemed to be recovering, at least outwardly, from the agitated dolorousness he carried into the sports-bar with him, as Brian endeavored to lift Jim's spirits with jocularity and, eventually, reasoning. Having elicited a few chortles from Jim, Brian began to grow more at ease himself, though, by this time, Jim's eyes were growing quite red. Jim had always been of relatively sober judgment, and yet, he seemed to be swimming in the grief of a glass enclosure upon which his head repeatedly butted. "I found this about a month ago, Brian."

"Found what?" Jim reached into his back pocket, but found nothing; he then realized that he had changed out of his work clothes and into the suit he was presently wearing, just before he and Sarah had severed for the evening, and shortly before he had called Brian from his phone. Jim then reached into his breast pocket and pulled out an opened envelope with a note inside of it. Jim read aloud, *"Please hurry; I have desired to see you. I don't know how much longer I can wait."*

"So what's it all about, Jim? Is *this* why you're so upset?

"Well wouldn't you be?"

"Man, I don't know; that seems like way too little to be this upset. Who wrote it?" Brian snatched the letter from Jim's hands, and he saw that it was addressed to Jim's wife, Sarah; it was signed, *"Paul."*

"Who's Paul?" Brian asked.

"I don't know."

"What did Sarah say about this?"

"Nothing."

"You mean you confronted her, and she simply refused to speak?"

With a beaten and humiliated expression, Jim bowed his heavy head and said,

"I haven't confronted her about it. I just started working late because I couldn't stand it... I couldn't stand the thought of it... the house I was saving for was only my excuse.... I put it in my suit so that I could spring it on her at dinner tonight... but that didn't happen."

A moment of awkward silence ensued. Not wishing to dwell on the exposed lie, Brian broke the silence by saying, "Wait, wait, wait; that letter could just be from some old boyfriend who looked up Sarah's address."

Jim pondered the suggestion for a moment, but he then replied, "Then, how would you account for the letter being addressed to Sarah, even though she now has my last name?" Brian spied the envelope quizzically.

"I just don't think you should rush to any conclusions yet. This envelope is only addressed to 'Sarah,' and it has no last name on it. Perhaps he found out what her last name had become and mailed the letter to that address in hopes that she might still be single."

"Single? — with a different last name?"

"Jenny left me a year ago, and she still has my last name."

"How do you know?"

"I looked her up..." Jim looked at Brian; "... but I never contacted her. Anyway, do you know any 'Pauls'?"

"No."

"Has Sarah ever talked about any 'Pauls' in her past?

"No."

"Look, you know I like to be realistic, but I also like to be as patient as I can. Why don't you just ask Sarah about it; you've never known her to lie before. If she is horsing around, she might just come clean about it."

"Or, if she *is* horsing around, *he* might just come clean about it."

"What do you mean, Jim?"

"I mean, 'Paul' was stupid enough to put his return address on the envelope." Another uncomfortable moment of silence grew between the two.

"Are you going to his house to confront him?" asked Brain. The redness of Jim's eyes deepened. "Do you want me to come along?"

"No thanks, Brian; I'll go this one alone," Jim said, as he gave the impression of a threatening volcano. Cooling for a second, Jim turned towards Brian and said, "Thanks for meeting me tonight; you're my best friend."

"Don't mention it. The drinks and appetizers are on me."

"I just hope the joke's not on me," replied Jim woefully. Brian had nothing to say. As Jim rose from his seat, Lisa spied his impending departure. Jim reached into his right, front pocket in order to dig out his keys, but he became pierced with fear when he remembered that he had left his keys — and Lisa's note — in the pair of pants that he had taken off and had thrown in the washing machine. Jim froze like an ice-sculpture whose forehead had begun to melt. In the heat of his argument with Sarah, he had forgotten to....

"What's wrong, Jim?" asked Brian. Jim hurried out of the sports-bar without saying anything more to anyone. Lisa appeared quizzically disappointed.

Jim ran. He bedewed his freshly pressed suit as he felt the pressure of too many loose ends begin to unravel the frayed remains of his marriage. Once Jim reached the corner of the sidewalk, he sprinted home in vain hopes of reaching the washing machine before Sarah, for he was unaware of the chronology that had been unfolded.

CHAPTER 21

Sarah sat motionless as she held the envelope that Tina had just handed her. Her heartache had been exchanged for bewilderment.

"Well, open it, Sarah," urged Tina. Sarah eyed the envelope curiously. After having paused for a moment, she tore the envelope's corner and proceeded to rip the entirety of a short side of the envelope from its remainder. Inside was a piece of folded paper; Sarah unfolded it. "What does it say?" asked Tina.

Sarah read aloud in a soft voice, "*I hope all is well with you. We agreed to get together at least once more. As I remember it, you informed me that you would contact me within a month's time. I have been waiting to see you. If it is within your power, please come to my house as soon as you can.*"

The letter was signed, "*Paul.*"

Tina's expression was wrought in perplexity, as if she were searching for something. Sarah's expression was fixed in guilt, and her emotions were becoming unraveled through the quivering exhalations that precede tacit tears. Then, Tina's eyes lightened; she raised her view in time to see Sarah begin to crumple under the heaviness of the situation. Tina scooted towards her slumping friend and caught her before Sarah's wet cheeks met dry reality, alone.

"I'm pregnant, Tina."

"What (!)? Have you told Jim?"

"No," Sarah whispered through a sniffle; "I was going to spring it on him tonight at dinner, but that didn't happen."

"Are you going to see Paul?"

Sarah sniffled again, but then she sobbed, though she managed to choke out a garbled, "Yes."

CHAPTER 22

"I can't believe how stupid I am!" Jim scolded himself. Nearly out of breath, Jim reached his apartment building. He noticed that his window was dark and that Sarah was not home. Guilty fear grew more forcefully in his chest. He was locked out of his home, and he had no idea where his wife had gone — with possible knowledge of the secret he had locked within his heart. Jim contemplated where Sarah could be. Amidst his panic, Jim forgot he was carrying a phone, and he began to run back to the sports-bar in hopes of catching Brian before he returned to his own, empty home.

☐ ☐ ☐

Sweating profusely from his run, Jim reentered the sports-bar. Lisa curled a surprised and hopeful smile upon Jim's reentry; after having stuffed her pad of paper inside her snake-skin belt, she approached him with a captivating smoothness.

"I was hoping that you'd come back," said Lisa in a low voice.

"Hi, Lisa," panted Jim in an attempt to regain his breath.

"She's not being good to you, is she? Wanna talk about it, Jimmy?" said Lisa, with scintillating eyes.

After having hesitated for a moment, having considered for a moment, having looked at her alluring presence for a moment, Jim reconstellated his focus and replied, "Maybe another time, Lisa."

"I'm starting to think you don't like me anymore, Jimmy," said Lisa as she stroked her hair and moved closer towards him. Jim's eyes darted back and forth as he silently scanned the room for Brian. "I'm starting to —"

"— Jim! What are you doing back here?" asked Brian as he emerged from the men's room. "You look like you just ran a marathon." Jim left Lisa standing in her pose, motioned for Brian to follow him, and the two stepped outside.

"Brian, I'm locked out... Sarah's not home... can you drive me somewhere?" An almost instantaneous, adrenaline-produced grin grew on Brian's face.

"Let's get him." Jim nodded in agreement, and the two of them walked outside and towards Brian's car. Lisa stood with a cold expression as she watched Jim exit as quickly as he had reentered.

Brian and Jim strode across the slick parking lot and approached Brian's car. Brian tipped his head back, took a swig, let out an exited howl, whipped his bottle across the parking lot, and unlocked his car. Jim knew Brian before and after....

"I'll drive, Brian."

Brian paused and glanced at Jim blankly. "O.K., Jimmy-boy... anything for a pal."

CHAPTER 23

Though the actual rainfall had halted, the evening air was filled with a cool spray and a slithering chill. The streetlights gleamed with individual halos in the misty night. The dense, moist air caused the traffic-lights to blur into hazy circles.

Sarah drove with a forcefulness that was caused by too many conflicting emotions that sought ventilation all at once. She had never been to Paul's house, but she had looked up directions to the address before she left Tina's. The traffic-light before her turned red before she had noticed it, and she slid to a stop.

Sarah reread the directions as she waited for the stoplight to turn green. Everything appeared as though enveloped by dense, wet sadness. A car pulled up next to Sarah, and she inadvertently turned her eyes towards it. The young man in the driver's seat had a quirky smirk on his face as he shifted his view from the windshield before him to the young woman beside him in his passenger seat. The woman in his passenger seat laughed hysterically. In an instant, both the man and the woman heaved with seemingly innocent laughter, and in the midst of their gladness, the woman leaned to her left and planted an affectionate peck onto the young man's right cheek. Their laughter subsided into glowing smiles, and then they proceeded forward into the night at the allowance of the green light that Sarah had not noticed. Sarah heard a car behind her honk its horn. Embarrassed, frustrated, and caught off guard, she drove forward into tearful obscurity.

As she drove, Sarah began to ponder the erosion between her and her young husband that had worn her to the reduced state in which she found herself. Her home felt vacant. Her car felt empty. Her life felt drained.

"How could I have been so stupid?" she asked herself out loud. Sarah drove through the rain; she felt ashamed, funereal, confused, pulled by conflicting strings that tugged asymmetrically and with varying vehemence. Her car sped for an hour towards the address on the torn envelope. It was 9:45 p.m., and Sarah felt the weight of guilt tick against her with increasing pressure. "I should have worked things out with him..." she thought. "How could all of this happen?"

□□□

Sarah neared her destination and thought, "I should have come here a long time ago." Though she lived in the city, she was only about an hour away from the mountains, and it appeared that Paul's home stood atop, or amongst, one of the many peaks before her. As her rusty car climbed the ascending road, the fog that had hung just above the ground in her city home now enshrouded the high road on which she drove. On clear days, the mountainous terrain was usually crowned with fog from evening until morning, but the sun's loftier stances always dispersed the mists from late morning to early evening. However, on cool, rainy days, the mountains remained bedecked with a shady, gray fog that swirled like languidly curling smoke.

Sarah felt her ears begin to pop. She heard and reheard Jim's sharpness ring in her unwanted recollection. She pictured Paul. As she proceeded up the ever-narrowing, winding road, she felt overwhelmed by the quiet isolation, with the exception of the little reminder in her belly. For all of the fighting that she had engaged with Jim, she felt as though she remained unheard; she thought to herself that if she stopped her car, got out, and screamed as loudly as she could, she would be met with the same indifferent result in the apparent wilderness she now found herself within. A sudden wave of fearful loneliness rippled through her chest. She drove for another 20 minutes. No rain fell, but the sky threatened to burst forth at any moment.

□□□

She came to a small, dirt road that turned off from the paved street on which she had been driving. The dirt road before her became increasingly difficult to see; suddenly, her headlights reflected off of a metal gate only 20 feet before her, and she skidded to a complete halt. The wrought-iron gate stood locked before her, and it was evident that the only purpose for the narrow, dirt road on which she had been driving was to serve as a driveway for the house at the end of it.

The wrought-iron gate was connected to a long, spiky, iron fence that wrapped around the property, and the house within the metal circular fence could barely be seen since a natural fence of very tall and very old trees stood sturdily erect just inside of the iron fence. She saw no lights.

Sarah's car sat before the gate and beside what appeared to be an old intercom system from her grandfather's days. She rolled down her window, leaned her arm out into the cool, moist night and pressed the white button that had become yellowed with age. She sat. She regretted. She feared.

"Yes?" said a voice on the intercom speaker.

"It's me, Sarah Davis... uh... Sarah Peters." There was a long and uncomfortable pause that recast the former silence upon Sarah and reinforced the churning of her nervous stomach. She thought to herself, "What if Jim comes home before I do?" Her stomach knotted itself with a pinching sensation.

The gates drew apart by some electrically controlled machinery.

"Pull up to the porch, my dear," said Paul's voice.

□□□

"Please come in," said Paul. Sarah entered Paul's house with a weariness she could no longer conceal. Her make-up was smeared on account of her tears; her hair was wet; her eyes were tired....

"You look beautiful, Sarah."

"You're so kind, Paul."

He held out his arms to receive her.

CHAPTER 24

"If he's touched her, I swear I'll...."
Jim and Brian sped through the damp night. The
thick mist hovered just above the ground like a
smoke-screen. Brian, warmed by his cold ones,
and Jim, heated with a mixture of embarrassment
and rage, raced through the night in Brian's car
without giving much attention to the rather ominous
surroundings that melded the street with the fog
upon a dark horizon.

□□□

Jim and Brian began their ascent up the
mountain. They then came to the small, dirt road
and turned onto it. The path became narrower and
darker, as there were no more streetlights to guide
their ride. Their surroundings grew blacker as they
drew nearer to their destination. The fog met the dirt
road and compelled them to slow down. Jim and
Brian drove into the increasingly concealing haze that
encircled the mountain road.

With the suddenness that Sarah had
experienced, Jim and Brian saw their headlights
reflect off of the iron gates before them, and they

slid to a stop. The gates hung open. However, two intimidating statues stood at either side of the open gate doors, and their poses were sculpted in a rather frightful manner. Jim and Brian gazed at the strange sculptures with uneasiness. In an attempt to conceal his gulp, Jim turned to observe Brian's reaction to the strange setting.

"This must be it," said Brian, as he pointed towards the house that was enshrouded by the thick fog. Jim and Brian's heat began to cool with discomfort as they realized that this "Paul" must be some iconoclast.

"48 Molten Mirror Drive; this is it," said Jim in response to Brian. "Do we just drive in?" Brian spied his surroundings with squinted eyes; the terrain was difficult to see because of its peculiar design, especially since it was encapsulated in the mist of the cool, wet evening.

"Go for it, Jim; there's two of us... ya know what I mean?" Brian urged; he was no stranger to trouble, and he had seen many a battlefield more uncertain than some private citizen's front lawn. As the two drove through the open gates, they noticed the enormous size of the front lawn on either side of them. The snaking driveway cut an uneven pattern through nearly two acres of the front lawn that was slightly speckled with large trees. "Look!" said Brian, though he kept his body still and did not dare to move in any sudden way. The two men noticed large, shadowy figures that stood eerily in the night, on the lawn, and that faced their car. Jim inadvertently stopped the car and found himself frozen and without the slightest notion as to what he and Brian should do. The figures were imposing, and they appeared to be frozen in a gaze that was transfixed on the car; their faces could not be seen from Brian's car, nor did their eyes flash, since they stood on either side of the driveway and not before the car's headlights.

"Douse the lights!" Brian whispered vehemently, almost annoyed with Jim's inexperience and indiscretion. Jim dipped down lower in his seat and continued to peer through the moist windows at the unflinching guards who stared back at Brian and him fixedly. As Brian's and Jim's eyes began to adjust to the extinguished headlights, they realized that they were beholding life-sized, and beyond life-sized, statues of animals, people, and polymorphic figures. The statues were of an enormity and peculiarity that would have set anyone's spine in rigidity and anyone's eyes in wonderment. The two beheld a life-sized statue of a man that stood next to two statues of oversized fish. To the right of the man was a statue that had a goat's head, and to the right of the goat was a statue that had a quadruped's lower-body. As Jim and Brian gazed around, they noticed a dozen of these large statues, and the two perplexed men both shot each other quizzical glances that produced two total upturned eyebrows between the two of them. Brian took his hand out of his breast pocket.

They proceeded, with the headlights off, towards the end of the driveway, until they came to a stop and parked next to Sarah's car. Brian's eyes widened and he turned to look at Jim. Jim's eyes quivered with a disturbed liquidity, and his hands exposed a slight tremor. "I knew it! I knew she was a little —"

"— Keep it down," Brian, whispered; he had recently come out of his entranced state. Brian pointed towards a lit, first-floor window in the large, decaying house that stood somewhat uphill from the driveway, but which was connected to a garage on the level of the driveway beneath the large-first-floor porch. Jim turned the car off, observed the window, turned back towards Brian, and the two friends said to each other simultaneously, "Let's go."

When the two arose from the car, they stood before a large trellis that was constructed in the form of a tunnel, about 12 feet tall, about 12 feet wide, and about 24 feet long. Old vines hung from the top of the trellis and snaked around the wooden posts that supported the seemingly slithering ceiling. A slight jolt waved through Jim, while Brian stood fast. Jim, full of wonder, anger, excitement, and inconsolableness, stood before the dark passage.

"Jim!" Brian whispered; "Let's do this thing; come on!" Brian continued, as he began to disappear into the shadows beneath the trellis that led towards the entrance.

Upon reaching the end of the trelliswork, the two men stood at the bottom of six steps; atop the steps were four marble faces that resembled the statues that occupied the front gateway. The faces were suspended above the floor and before the threshold of the front door.

CHAPTER 25

The front door flung open.

"Brian (!)?"

"Hello, Sarah," sneered Brian, who stood ready and alert in the living-room with war-hardened fists. "Jim!"

"Sarah!" stormed Jim, who pulsed with indignation. "Where is he? Where is this 'Paul?' Get out here, Paul!" Jim shouted, as he stood in hot rage. As Brian, Sarah, and Jim all stood in a tension of ignorance and fear, three silent seconds slipped past. Jim could hear his rapid heartbeat pound like kettle drums in his ears. Jim's chest heaved, and his fists twitched. Then, a gray-haired senior citizen, adorned with a purple-scarlet robe, emerged through the doorway with both of his hands occupied with cups of steaming coffee.

"Hello, Jim," said Paul.

Totally taken aback, Jim, with wide, confusion-filled eyes, exclaimed, "*You're* Paul?"

Somewhat bewildered, Paul replied, "I always have been; Paul Gephen, at your service."

"Gephen... Gephen? — the 'Mr. Gephen' who married Sarah and me? Your first name is 'Paul?'"

"It has been, as long as I can remember, Mr. Davis." Having turned towards Sarah, Paul continued, "That is your last name now, right Sarah? I have a hard time remembering things these days, my dear; I always think of you under your Grandfather's name... I mean your maiden name; that is the reason I mailed two letters to two different addresses. My memory has become as emblazoned as the sunset," he regretted. "I feel as though many recollections are beginning to blend and to melt..." Paul sighed with a weak yet heavy exhalation. "I thought your last name had become 'Davis,' but my memory of your wedding has become somewhat decolored, though my memory of you has not. I remember how proud your father was when you were born"; Paul smiled with a soft fondness; "I remember holding you when you were a month old; I remember holding your father in my arms when he was a month old."

"Let's get him, Jim!" exclaimed Brian, as he rapidly advanced towards Paul.

"Whoa, whoa, Brian; relax. I screwed up and jumped to a false conclusion... again. 'Paul' married Sarah and me, remember? I only met him on the day of our wedding — as 'Mr. Gephen'; I didn't know his first name, and I didn't really care at the time; oh... no offense, Mr. Gephen."

"None taken," replied Paul. With a mystified decrease in vigor, Brian began to chuckle, then to laugh, then to grow exceedingly annoyed.

"Jim?" Jim turned and looked at Brian. "The next time you want to come into the bar all busted-up inside just so that you can pull on my heart-strings in hopes that I'll go chasing creepy stone animals in some stranger's yard, do me a favor and drink in your own house!" Brian's expression was beyond cross, but then he erupted into hilarity as he slapped his thighs in laughter at Jim, wagged his head and muttered, "...you dope...." Jim began to laugh as well. Sarah's jaw hung open. Paul stood in his usual, tall, bow-chested manner.

"Would you gentlemen enjoy some coffee also?" In the midst of humiliating laughter and self-abasement, the two relaxing men coughed out their assent to Paul's offer. "Sit down, children; make yourself at home. I haven't had visitors in a long time."

CHAPTER 26

Paul, Sarah, Jim, and Brian all sat around Paul's coffee table. Paul leaned back into his aged sofa and sipped his coffee. Sara, Jim, and Brian all leaned forward in their seats, like basketball players on a bench, as the three found it a bit difficult to recline on account of the confusion their youthful vigor had brought into the home of a peaceful, seasoned gentleman. Paul continued to sip his coffee while the other three continued to hold theirs uneasily. Brian sat in fixed concentration, as he looked into his coffee cup, and as he put the pieces of the puzzle together mentally. Finally, breaking the silence, Sarah sheepishly said, “I'm so embarrassed….”

“So let me get this straight, Sarah…” Brian interrupted; “your dad's father was best friends with Mr. Gephen since before your dad was born? Mr. Gephen is also a chaplain?”

“Yes,” nodded Sarah. “Yes, but I have never been to Mr. Gephen's house before; he was my *grandfather's* best friend.” Paul smiled nostalgically as he sipped his coffee. “I saw him when I went to my grampa's house as a kid, but my grampa and him would always be talking about ancient stuff. It just seemed to me like Gramps and Mr. Gephen were always talking about stuff I had no clue about. I would just say, 'Hi,' to him before I hugged my grampa, but Mr. Gephen was always kind enough to shake my hand."

"You used to let me hug you when you were a baby, Sarah..." Paul chuckled, "...before you could speak, anyway," he smiled. Sarah hung her head. "Oh, lighten up, my dear; that was all a long time ago."

"So then what?" asked Brian of Sarah, as he sipped his coffee. Having turned towards a silent Jim, Brian blurted sarcastically, "Are you getting this all down, Jimmy – huh (!)?" Jim gave a sheepish, tired grin.

"After Dad died in the car accident, when I was 19, I spent a lot more time around my grampa.

"What about your mom," asked Brian.

"She died in childbirth... when I was born."

"Oh..." said Brian, with a softer tone.

"When I told Gramps that I wanted to marry Jim, and that we were going to go to Las Vegas, Gramps made it quite clear that he wanted us to get married at his church. Jim and I really didn't want that, so Gramps urged us to get married at his house. It was all one big whirl. You remember how 'last-minute' everything was, Jim...."

"Yeah, and how I had saved a thousand bucks for the craps table too," Jim muttered softly. Paul tipped his head to let out a little, eye-rolling half-laugh.

"So, Jim and I were to be married at my grampa's house, in the backyard. Gramps said that Vegas was no place to enter into a 'holy covenant,' and he said that I needed, 'everything done properly, by a man of God.' I didn't care much, honestly; oh, no offense, Mr. Gephen."

"None taken, my dear," replied Paul.

"I just wanted to marry Jim." Her eyes began to well up. "So, we got married. I was just reveling in the whole thing, but, before we left for the honeymoon..."

"...in Vegas," Jim whispered to Brian.

"...Mr. Gephen asked that I promise to contact him one month after our marriage; that was over two years ago. I just forgot," Sarah said remorsefully.

"...and I lost a grand," said Jim regretfully.

"I knew you would," said Paul confidently, to himself.

"So," said Brian, "Mr. Gephen, here, was your grandfather's best friend. You only saw him every now and then, as a kid. Your mom died in childbirth; your dad died in a car accident when you were 19. Your dad's dad got Mr. Gephen to marry the two of you.

"Yeah," said Sarah, as her eyes gazed into her coffee cup.

"About a month after your wedding," Brian continued, "you were supposed to contact Mr. Gephen, but that was over two years ago... and you never did. Since then, poor Mr. Gephen has been sitting here by the phone in this house waiting for you to call and visit. More than two years later, about a month ago, he sent a letter addressed to 'Sarah,' signed 'Paul' to your apartment that you now live in with Jim; since he got no response, he sent another letter to Tina's apartment addressed to you under your maiden name, 'Sarah Peters.' Jim got the first letter before you did, and he thought you had become special friends with the mailman; then he retreated into his little, non-communicative shell like he always does. Tina, like a true space-cadet, forgot to give you the second letter, for nearly two weeks, until tonight. Meanwhile, Jim got all bent out of shape, started working late for about a month, and came crying to me tonight. Just before he came into Lisa's... uhh... Malik's Sports Bar, the two of you geniuses got into a fight, and you, Sarah, went to Tina's, where she gave you the letter. Your guts were already in knots, you didn't know what to do, and you were so upset, that you came driving all the way out here. On the flipside, Jim's wonderful memory made him come back to Malik's, got me all fired up, and had the two of us come out to this house. When we thought we were about to get shot by the enemy, we realized we were on the property of someone who likes statues. We busted in here ready for action and found you innocently hanging out with the guy who married you — who was your grandfather's best friend. Do I have the story right?"

"Yes," answered Jim and Sarah in simultaneous humiliation.

"I need to get some new friends," replied Brian, as he shook his head.

Paul raised an eyebrow and said, "Children, I hope I haven't caused you any grief; I'm quite sorry if I have."

Not allowing Jim and Sarah to answer, Brian blurted, "None at all, Mr. Gephen; I haven't had this much fun since the war...." Jim grew an ashamed-looking smirk, and Sarah's expression mirrored Jim's. "If you don't mind, Jimmy-boy, I'm going home now to sleep this off, and I'm going to pretend you have a brain. Give me a call if the two of you ever need something — legitimate. Next time, talk it out between the two of you before you rope me into anything." Brian stood up, leaned towards Paul, extended his right hand and said, "Thanks for the coffee, Sir."

"Don't mention it. Please feel free to visit me any time," replied Paul kindly; with that, Brian made his way towards the door, and past the purple-heart medal that hung on the wall.

"Would you like to rest here, soldier?" Paul asked Brian.

"Yes, sir; but I think it's better if I go. I think Jimmy and Sarah need to talk with you, alone. Thank you. Good night." Brian stepped out into the cool, damp, night, and he shut the door behind him in his usual, abrupt manner.

"Quite a colorful friend you two have," said Paul. The three of them watched Brian from the picture-window as he cautiously approached one of the lawn statues, which was nearly enshrouded in fog under the clouded, mid-night sky; his right hand was in the left breast-pocket of his jacket. Brian made a couple of quick, jabbing gestures at the stone lion with his left hand, shrugged his shoulders, gave Leo a quick pet, removed his right hand from his breast pocket, got into his car, and drove off into the mist.

Sarah shook her head.

"It seems like he hasn't made the adjustment yet," remarked Paul.

CHAPTER 27

Paul, Jim, and Sarah sat back down
following Brian's departure. The three picked up their
cups and continued to drink what was left of their
coffee. Jim spied his surroundings. The house had
an air of antiquity about it. The walls were almost
completely concealed by bookshelves that were replete
with countless volumes which had become worn with
obvious use. Behind the bookshelves hung wallpaper
that looked to be from Sarah's grandfather's
generation; the light fixtures and decorations
appeared to be of the same era.

The furniture gave the impression that it was
once lush and elegant, but that over 50 years had
worn plush comfort into a vestige that suggested
happier times. The manner of decoration and the
articles within the home seemed to increase in age
with each of Jim's glances; the style of the house
itself appeared to be over a century old. The vast
number of books that almost wallpapered the walls
contained writings that were written centuries, and
in some cases millennia, ago; even these appeared
recent when compared to the various scrolls that were
locked within an assortment of glass boxes that stood

upon decorative pedestals. A faint hint of mold mixed with coffee and tobacco could be detected.

Celestial and terrestrial globes of varying sizes rested upon a large desk. Paintings of ancient landscapes hung in the few places where bookcases did not stand. Another large and impressive desk was covered with various maps that gave testament to having been rolled up for quite some time, though one of these maps was held open by two non-English dictionaries that weighed down either end of it.

In the midst of the nearly archaic surroundings, Paul leaned back into his soft sofa and said, "Why don't the two of you spend the night here at my house? It's quite late, and by this time, the fog is thick; besides, we're all tired, and it seems that you two have been on quite an unpleasant adventure."

Sarah looked at Jim, shrugged her shoulders and replied, "Are you sure, Paul?"

Paul smiled warmly and replied, "Please, be my guest. I have a spare bedroom in which the bed is made. When you two wake up, I'll make you breakfast."

Sarah turned towards her weary husband and asked, "Would that be alright, Jim?"

"Sure, Sarah... yeah, that's fine," stammered Jim.

"Then it is settled," said Paul. "I have a robe for you to wear, Mr. Davis, but I'm afraid I haven't any clothes for you, Sarah."

"Oh, don't worry about it. I have an overnight-bag in the car." Jim's chest felt as if it had caved internally. Paul pretended not to notice the awkwardness of Sarah's comment and the perceived sting betrayed by Jim's reaction.
Jim, embarrassed and surprised, attempted to smooth the situation by saying, "I'll help you, Sarah."

"That's alright; I can get it myself," she said disinterestedly, as she headed for the door. Sarah opened the front door, stepped over the old threshold, walked past the stone guardians of the door, down the steps, and disappeared under the coiling vines.

Jim was left standing before Paul, and he did not know how to react, what to say, or how to feel. Paul broke the uneasy silence by asking, "Jim, why don't you relax and sit down. Can I get you anything?"

"No, sir; I'm fine, thank you. Uhhh... I'm, uhhh... really sorry about barging in here tonight, I thought Sarah was...."

"You needn't even say it; I understand. We have all of tomorrow to discuss it. For now, just be relieved that your suspicions were false, and that your wife is true."

"Thank you, Sir."

"Call me 'Paul'; I'll get your room ready for you, Mr. Davis."

"Call me 'Jim.'"

"I'll return briefly, Jim."

"Ok, Mr., uhh, Paul." Paul produced another warm smile and sauntered down the hallway towards the spare bedroom to make it ready for the young couple to close their eyes together for a change.

CHAPTER 28

Paul returned from the spare bedroom, and Sarah returned from her car outside. Jim and Sarah were led down a dim hallway. The creaky floor disturbed the stillness of the night. The walls of the hallway were decorated with various framed pictures. Faded black-and-white military photos of men in their late teens and early twenties were fastened to the walls in such a manner as if history itself had been suspended. Hand-painted Hebrew calligraphy hung on the walls within frames that resembled doorways. Miniature maps of the ancient world stood behind glass that seemed to encapsulate bygone times.

"Here we are," said Paul. "Unless there is anything else that befits this evening, I wish the two of you a good night."

"I think we're fine," Jim replied wearily.

"Thank you so much, again, Paul," added Sarah; with that, Paul gave a smiling nod and left Jim and Sarah at the door as he walked back the way he came, down the dim hallway, and disappeared silently around the corner.

Jim and Sarah stood alone in the old, spare bedroom and prepared themselves for slumber. The air was thick with tension. They had not slept in the same room for a while. Jim was uncertain as to whether or not Sarah had found the letter that he had accidentally left in his pocket along with his keys. Jim pondered the possibility that, perhaps, Sarah had packed her overnight bag and headed for Tina's house merely as a result of the fight they recently had.

Sarah pretended to ignore Jim as she busied herself between the bed and the little powder-room that was attached to the corner of the bedroom. She felt bruised, crushed, humiliated, indignant.... She contemplated how her otherwise "honest" husband had become involved with some strange woman. It seemed, according to the story they had all corporately deduced in Paul's living-room, that the only reason Jim began working late was because of his suspicions of her; however, such a story did not explain the note she pulled out of Jim's pants. Jim stood awkwardly in the robe Paul had lent him; it held a smoky scent, and it fit Jim quite well.

"Did she find the note?" Jim thought to himself. His heart beat quickly. "No, she couldn't have. She left just after I did, right? Yeah, that's right. Why would she check the laundry?" he continued to wonder. Then, in paralyzing remembrance, he recalled how if he had, indeed, left his keys in the pocket of his pants, the keys would have banged loudly enough inside the dryer to have aroused anyone's attention... that is, if Sarah had actually done the laundry after he left. "Of course she didn't," he thought to himself. "Yeah, she's always tidying up and all, but she didn't do any laundry today... no way...." Jim stood rigidly, but he attempted to appear relaxed. "I love you, Sarah," he said softly. Sarah emerged from the powder room.

"What?"

"I love you," Jim repeated. Sarah produced a mixture of a frown and a smile that took up residence at either corner of her lips respectively. She slowly walked over to the bed, and Jim followed her. In silence, the two of them sat down on the bed together.

After an uncomfortable moment of consideration, Sarah replied, "I love you too, Jim." The knots in Jim's chest and stomach began to loosen. The clenched muscles in his nervous throat began to relax. His heartbeat, which had been pounding in his ears, began to pulse into quietude once again. The tiny beads of sweat that had congregated just below his hairline began to dry. His wife was truly a lovely person, lovely to behold, and lovely to hold. Jim advanced towards his prize, his bride, his hope, and as he opened his arms to her, she quietly asked, "Who is she, Jim?"

CHAPTER 29

Jim attempted to answer his wife's question with as much straightforwardness, honesty, and simplicity as he could, but before he could finish his first sentence, Sarah erupted by exclaiming,

"Lisa (!)? Who's Lisa (!)?"

"Sarah! Wait... please calm down, let me —"

"—So *this* is where you've been for a month? You're always 'working overtime' or at that sports bar visiting '*Brian*,'" sneered Sarah, with a wounded blend of pain and contempt. She arose from her fatigued, sitting position on the bed next to her red-faced husband with a renewed vigor that was incapable of full strength, but capable enough for a full fight and a full termination of what she and Jim referred to as a marital "contract."

"Please! — keep it down, Sarah; he'll hear us (!); it's past midnight!" Jim growled with a whisper's equivalency to a shout. He rose with an attempt to place comforting, quieting hands upon his faithful wife.

"Don't touch me! Don't..." Sarah streamed with raging tears, "...ever touch me! How could you? How could you!"

"It's not what you think..."

"...this 'marriage' isn't what *you* think! I want a
—"

"— Stop! Let me explain —"

"— DIVORCE!"

The room was cold and quiet, full of furniture
and pictures, but empty and dying. Jim backed
away, aghast, tearfully aghast... his mouth hung
open as if in an attempt to drink from a fire-hose...
his hands trembled as much as the tears that clung
to each other before Sarah's reddened eyes. Quietly,
in a reduced, sapped manner, Jim backed away from
his wife without being conscious of it, until his back
thudded against the aged walls of the room. Sarah
beheld her husband, who had longed to hold her,
attempt to stand as he slid his back, against his will,
down the wall until he sat in slumped subjection to
melancholy. The paradox of a weighted void stood
upon the place where his heart had once beat.
Looking straight ahead into winding thoughts of
nothingness, Jim whispered softly, "Sarah?" just in
time to hear the light switch twitch and to behold
darkness envelope the two young "lovers."

"Stay away from me. I'm leaving in the
morning," said Sarah.

"It's not what you think," whispered Jim.

CHAPTER 30

"I do."

Do you, Jim Davis, take this woman to be your wife, to have and to hold...."

"I do."

"You may now kiss the bride." Jim lifted Sarah's veil, tipped her chin delicately, and, with closed eyes, beheld a growing glow. Jim's eyes clenched more tightly, and his arms shut around her. The light intensified. The silence was deafening, the light was blinding. The streams of morning sunlight woke Jim from his dreamy memory, and as he sat up from the floor, he turned to see the bed empty and made up.

"Sarah?" Jim said with a startled voice. "Sarah?" Jim arose to a dark, yet shining morning. Panic's claws clutched Jim's chest and evoked a panting that, with each hurried breath, dissolved Jim's dreamy memory of his wedding and ushered in his growing dread; fear and anguish were engaging a wrenching tug-of-war contest within Jim's chest.

Jim darted out of the spare-bedroom door and down a hallway that became increasingly unfamiliar. Having reached the hallway's corner, the passage turned opposite of what he had remembered from the previous night; nevertheless, he ran, fueled by horrid emotions he could not articulate. The dim hallway grew brighter. Jim ran into a spacious room. He stopped, jerked his head to and fro desperately; upon his second "to," the image of Paul and Sarah materialized in his awakening eyes.

"Don't be in such a hurry, Jim; breakfast won't be ready for another ten minutes. It is easier to park a car at two miles per hour than it is at 50 miles per hour," said Paul. "Sit down with your wife. Would you like some coffee while breakfast cooks?"

Mystified and uneasy, Jim replied with a simple, "Sure." Jim was confused, but he exhaled with a hint of temporary relaxation; "Yeah, that would be great," he continued.

Sarah sat stoically and spoke a simple, "Good morning, Jim."

"Good morning, Honey," replied Jim, as he leaned over and smooched Sarah's forehead, and as she drew her head backwards slightly.

CHAPTER 31

Paul, Jim, and Sarah sat around the breakfast table, and only Paul appeared at ease. Sarah endeavored to paint a phony smile over her obvious crossness. Jim attempted to pretend to be relaxed, though all he wanted to do was to get Sarah alone and out of Paul's earshot in order to tell her everything he had on his mind and heart. The tension was obvious, though Paul was considerate and carried himself with a nonchalant pleasantness.

"How is the food, you two?"

"Wonderful, Mr.... Paul," replied Jim.

"Delicious," answered Sarah.

"Good... I am relieved that you two have made good on your word," said Paul.

"What word?" asked Jim, as he looked back and forth between his wife and Paul.

"The day I married you two lovebirds, you gave me your word that you would visit me."

Both Jim and Sarah bowed their heads a bit, and then resurfaced with a simultaneous, "Sorry."

"Don't mention it," said Paul with a caring, gravelly voice. "On another note... you know, it can be quite a destructive practice to prohibit one from finishing one's sentences. Often, it is a closed ear that leads to a closed heart, and to answer before hearing is both folly and shame."

Feeling convicted by her trifling attitude towards her former agreement, Sarah spoke in a soft voice and said, "Paul, I'm really sorry that we didn't arrange a get-together when we agreed to do so."

"Sarah, sometimes forgiveness can be perceived in a smile, and I have been smiling since long before you two made good on your word last night. Thank you for coming to my home." Paul radiated warmth towards the pair, and, with an air of encouragement, he continued to say, "I have hardly ever seen a better fit for two people than you two. Do you have any children?"

"No," Jim responded.

"You know, it can be almost humorous to watch children play with toy tools, even though the children have no idea how to utilize the real tools their toys represent. So long as children continue in their efforts together, it is amazing what sort of relationship can be produced. I remember the first time I banged my finger with a hammer... and it is strange how both pain and joy can paint the eyes with the same transparent pink.

"It seems to me that the gifts given to us are not given in a developed form; rather, it seems that our capabilities are like seeds that, through proper cultivation and nourishment, eventually produce the

intended design that the Gift-giver had in mind. At
the same time, a lack of labor and support appears
to stifle and, sometimes, to destroy a gift outright.
Would you agree?"

The young couple sat motionless and
perplexed. "Yeah... I guess so," said Sarah.

"I can see where you're coming from," Jim
added.

"Well, who ever takes one stab with a shovel,
throws seed into the hole, and shouts, 'Grow!' to any
worthwhile effect? Every form of enduring goodness
is worth waiting for; the problem is that children,
young and old, often deem the worthwhile to be
worthless and the worthless to be worthwhile. It is
ironic how a lack of patience is proven foolish by the
passage of time.

"When questions are not asked, the imagination
can become quite an adversary. When the wrong
questions are asked, unsuitable answers await.
When the right questions are asked, the common
practice of not allowing another to finish his or her
words only shows a lack of patience." Sarah cleared
her throat. Paul continued: "So often, ideas are
developed in haste because one responded without
hearing the totality of a matter, and such hastened
ideas often usher in misunderstandings based upon
false foundations that can collapse any house no
matter how strongly the house itself may be built."
Jim swallowed. Paul took a sip of his drink and

asked, "Do you have any idea how many times I have married two people who put the cart before the horse and expected to get *pulled* to happiness?" asked Paul.

"What do you mean?" asked Sarah.

"Have you ever seen a bug-zapper, Sarah?"

"Sure."

"I have always marveled at the fact that 1,000 bugs fly happily into incandescence because they are attracted to it, and how all of those 1,000 bugs find themselves burned. It is even more astonishing to ponder the 1,001st bug as it flies toward the same fate. Sure, people are inclined to attempt to embrace what is attractive, but putting consideration second to passion often produces a glowing dream that never materializes into anything beyond a burn." Jim found a piece of food caught in his throat; Sarah crossed her ankles in feminine elegance. "Please tell me again how the two of you met," requested Paul; "it is so wonderful to hear tales about the seeds of love."

CHAPTER 32

Paul poured grape juice for Jim and Sarah as they ate breakfast. Jim and Sarah were both taken off-guard by the smoothness of the juice, and Sarah stated that it was, by far, the best she had ever tasted; Jim concurred. Despite the obvious tension between Jim and Sarah, breakfast continued decently. Paul's kindness softened much of the pain that pinched the innards of the young couple, and so sweet was his demeanor that Sarah found it easy, at times, to forget her troubles, so long as Paul engaged her.

Paul gave detailed accounts of Sarah's grandfather in the days before her own father was born, and his recollection was, at times, so precise (though intermittently so) that, even though her grandfather had been deceased for years, she felt as though he was alive and could be called upon readily. Sarah drank in Paul's words as readily as she did his wonderful grape juice.

Paul evinced a craving for details, and his reflections were painted by minute, but significant, descriptions that pointed his listeners towards an eventual whole that would not have made much sense unless the necessarily descriptive groundwork had been laid. It seemed, at first, that Paul spoke in riddles, but the number of them and the order in which they were presented ultimately materialized into flowing accounts that Sarah and Jim had, otherwise, only been the recipients of the conclusions of those very accounts. That is, Sarah (and to a lesser extent, Jim) had heard many of these stories concerning Sarah's father's father before, though they formerly had little clue as to why those stories were meaningful, as such accounts had once seemed to be the mere ramblings of yesteryear. The morning began to darken.

Paul proved puzzling. His manner of speaking was precise, though the way in which he connected topics appeared, at first glance, to be somewhat random. It required patience to appreciate the chaplain's words. However, there was a shade of poignancy that tinted his speech, for it was evident that his mind had begun to suffer time's cruelties, as Paul sometimes encountered lapses that caused him to struggle with certain specifics, though hair-splitting detail was a ceaseless component of his words. Both Sarah and Jim could tell that Paul had an inclination towards precision, but that this inclination was in the process of battling the erosion that was penetrating his memory. Nevertheless, Paul's memories of Sarah's grandfather were both humorous and tear-provoking, as he expounded upon subjects that ranged from innocent, youthful blunders to the death of Sarah's grandmother, her son, and her son's wife; for Sarah's grandfather had suffered the loss of his wife, only child, and his daughter-in-law in his own lifetime. However, Paul avoided landing his stories in the lap of forlornness, and he always provided some ray of hope or humor to paint a charming, accurate ending.

"Thank you so much for a wonderful breakfast, Paul," said Sarah.

"It was my pleasure," Paul replied.

"Yeah, really; breakfast was great," chimed Jim.

"Again, thank you so much for everything," Sarah said, as she began to rise from her chair.

"Please don't tell me that you are leaving so soon. I have been so anxious to see the two of you together.... It is only Saturday morning, and not even 9:30 yet."

Sarah instantly realized her ingratitude. "Oh... I'd love to stay, Paul; I just need to wash my hands." Sarah excused herself and walked over to the kitchen sink to wash her hands for no reason.

"Jim?"

"Yes, Paul."

"Do you know that you have married an absolute gem?"

With a deep sigh of memory mixed with hope, Jim dreamily and tiredly replied in a soft, nearly broken voice, "Yes, sir; I know."

Paul produced another warm smile of memory mixed with hope, and the two of them finished what was left of their breakfast to the tune of the sink Sarah had turned on for what seemed to be an overabundant span. Sarah made certain to keep her back to the two men as she intended on stopping the flow of water the instant her eyes dried. Jim spied his young, lovely wife splashing water onto her face — in the kitchen sink — in a failed attempt to be discrete. Paul pretended not to notice anything beyond the savor of the breakfast and the pleasure his company afforded him.

CHAPTER 33

Though Paul's house was very organized, Jim and Sarah perceived that the majority of Paul's time was devoted to the books within it as opposed to the structure itself. Paul's house seemed rather large for a gentleman of his age to live in by himself. Something about the possessions in Paul's home, combined with the grounds that surrounded the house, exuded an air of oldness and newness held in harmony by some unexplained mystery wrought in the secrets of bygone love.

Paul was draped in his regal-looking robe, and he gave the impression of having been a strapping, valiant man in the shrinking past. However, his frame had much succumbed to time's indifference, and his sunken eyes said that he was near to entering the way of all the world. His breathing seemed erratic, for there were times when he would string sentences together effortlessly as if he had memorized them from some book, but there were other times when he appeared weary and almost out of breath in mid sentence. Paul impressed the two young lovers as being an animate paradox; whatever was inside of him was much larger than what his physical, withering frame suggested.

In an apparently random manner, Paul began an unanticipated conversation: "I find it interesting that the ancient Babylonians called a collection of plants contained within pots 'gardens.' Did you know that the *Song of Songs* refers to woman in the context of a 'garden' and a 'paradise'?" Jim and Sarah looked at each other quizzically.

Sarah replied with a confused, "What?"

"Oh… never mind." Paul changed subjects rapidly again; "On another note, it is more than likely that ancient philosophy did not become systematically argumentative until it entered into Greece, and it is quite evident that the entirety of Plato's philosophy was not a novelty of his own, but it was largely a collection of ancient eastern traditions synthesized with a fresh originality. Anyway… what was I saying? Yes, yes…. Ancient education, particularly that of the easterners, was not so much disputative as it was inductively pointed towards the underlying truths ensconced beneath stories that, upon first glance, appeared incredible. Of course, the stories were often told in the format of riddles, epigrams, parables, proverbs, and other forms of related similitudes. The purpose of the seemingly impossible and enigmatic nature of the ancient stories was the craft of a deliberate design that exposed the devout and the profane. Those who were not devout were considered the same as those who did not seek wisdom. Those who were devout were understood to be those who sought after wisdom and its dark sayings." Jim's forehead was as wrinkled as Sarah's as the two pondered why Paul was now discussing something they were both ignorant of and cared nothing about; nevertheless, he continued. "The prevailing idea was that wisdom resided in the mind of God, and that God was the Great King. One of the most distinguishing marks of ancient, eastern Kings was their ability to propound and to untangle riddles. In fact, the Hebrew word for 'sublime, spiritual discourse' *is* a Hebrew word for 'riddle.'"

"Whoa... you mean that discussing spiritual matters was understood as discussing riddles?" asked Sarah.

"Certainly — which is why both ideas are the same word, in Hebrew," said Paul emphatically. "The process of attempting to decipher the logic behind riddles was, essentially, the ancient easterners' loftiest education. Deciphering the answer to the riddle elevated the student to a higher tier of learning whereupon the education could continue and the devotion of spiritual discourse would increase. If the stories themselves were only memorized and not decoded, the only thing a person had was a mass of accounts which, at first glance, seemed mostly impossible, if not altogether unbelievable." Then, in what seemed to be, again, a random statement, Paul continued by saying, "Please allow me the privilege of showing you my garden. We have many things to discuss, and the day is young, though it is growing cloudy.... It is amazing what can be learned from the silence of nature, and it is astounding what can be learned of people's silence as well. Eyes can surge louder than words, just as words can cut deeper than blades. Plants are pruned in order that they may produce more fruit, but all pruning requires the knife. An earring augments a lobe's beauty, though the ear must first be pierced." Seeing that he was losing his audience, Paul simply said, "Like I said, please let me show you my garden. Let's get dressed and grab our jackets."

□□□

The two young "lovers" were escorted to the back-porch of Paul's house. As they stepped onto the creaky porch, Jim and Sarah beheld a row of trees about 20 feet in front of them that appeared to bend into something circular towards the right and towards the left, in the manner of a round wall that bulged towards Paul's house. Either end of the bowed wall of trees melted into forest. There were no gaps between the branches of the trees, for the branches had grown in such close proximity to each other that the limbs of two trees occupied a single space so that the row of trees was truly impenetrable from about six feet high until their respective leafy apexes. The round wall of trees stood behind an equally round wall of thorn-bushes that had been planted quite closely to the tree trunks, and so closely to each other that they appeared as a spiky wreath.

There was an opening in the midst of the thorny hedge. The opening led to a space that existed between two trees. Large thorn-bushes grew in front of the two principle trees that defined the passageway, and the size of the passageway itself looked as if it could permit a car, though there was no concrete or dirt path made for automobiles.

Behind the passage that had been cut through the thorn-bushes, and between the two trees, were two metal gate doors. The doors were suspended upon an imposing stone wall that stood behind the wall of trees. This "garden" was no mere plantation; rather, it was more like a fortress, as it was evident that the owner of the garden had no desire for anyone to enter outside of his allowance. The stone wall was crowned with broken shards of colorful glass that had been cemented on top of it. The steadily darkening morning's fog hung just low enough to conceal the glass that crowned the wall.

Before the gates, and beside the two thorn-bushes on either side of the gates, stood two tall statues of an intimidating stature and daunting appearance. These statues appeared to be erected so as to serve as gate-keepers. They had the feet and horns of bulls, the bodies of lions, the faces of men, and their sides were covered with enormous wings. Each statue stood atop a pedestal that looked like a large wheel marked with the words, "Spring, Summer, Autumn, and Winter." Both statues held swords; but, the blades of the swords were carved so as to resemble flames that had what looked to be rounded double-u's etched all over them in a manner that looked like tongues of fire. A shining, bronze statue, which was nothing short of frightening, glinted above the lintel of the doorway.

"Come, children," beckoned Paul, as he sauntered towards the garden door, whose top was enveloped by a mist that glowed from the rising sun. Jim and Sarah turned towards each other and locked eyes in uneasiness. The two noticed that, despite the ascension of the sun before them, the sky was darkening behind them, as a storm threatened to lash the landscape.

"How well do you know this guy, Sarah?" Jim whispered.

"Hardly at all," she replied. Paul pulled a key from his pocket, unlocked the gates, stepped over the threshold, and was enveloped by a damp mist.

"Come, children..." said Paul, who stood out of sight, but just before the puzzled, cautious couple; "...we have much to discuss, and it seems as if time is not on our side," drifted Paul's faceless voice.

With imagination and hope knit together by emotion, the young couple crossed the threshold and journeyed into apparent opacity.

CHAPTER 34

Jim and Sarah had stepped into a curling haze. After turning this way and that way, Jim and Sarah realized that what appeared to be a few acres on the outside was actually an enormous piece of property of a size that escaped their collective estimation. They heard Paul's voice: "It is amazing what manner of resilience people will display when they feel enclosed. It is also amazing how those who make brave decisions often melt into cowardice when trouble comes and a path of escape seems to be an option." Paul, with his dark, sunken eyes, appeared through the mist to Jim and Sarah as they walked towards his rattling voice.

"What do you mean?" asked Sarah.

"After one has encountered an opposition, and there is no perceived escape, a combatant is often invigorated beyond normality to brave whatever onslaught might come his or her way. However, if there appears to be an open door of escape, those who once thought themselves intrepid often back-peddle towards what appears to be the only means of solution."

Puzzled by Paul's cryptic abruptness, but having apprehended the reason for his application, Sarah replied, "And what happens if they take what seems to be the easy way out?"

"They are often overcome by an unforeseen set of difficulties that await them in their retreat."

"So you're saying that all fights are worth fighting head-on?"

"No. You must choose your battles, and you must do so with discretion. I merely meant to indicate that once a commitment is engaged, that commitment should be kept with bravery and fortitude.

"It is foolish for one to battle with the one to whom he bound himself in covenant; the beauty of such a commitment is that the two covenanting parties are intended to brave hazy futures and scourging storms together, despite the opposition. Many young covenanting parties paint each other hazy pictures of fanciful aspirations because they do not understand covenants, for they only grasp contracts; and such an errant and unrealistic perception is often retaliated against with tempestuous words. Accordingly, the apparently discordant, bleak-looking futures and scourging storms are not braved by the covenanting parties, but are instead caused by them."

"Well then, how do you know what battles to choose to take on?"

Paul looked upon both Jim and Sarah in their uneasiness and said, "When you two stood before this garden, where your imaginations animated by the statues you saw?"

"Yes," replied Sarah.

"Sure," answered Jim.

"Were your emotions charged?" continued Paul.

"Yes," said Sarah.

"How far could you see past the gate?"

"I could hardly see anything," responded Jim.

"Me too," admitted Sarah.

"Did you cross the threshold together anyway?"

"Yes," acknowledged the two respectively.

"So you joined forces and braved the uncertain together?"

"Yes," Sarah answered. The two continued to stand uneasily and with expressions that combined uncertainty with curiosity.

"...and standing in the midst of an uncertainty larger than what you had anticipated, and hoping to reach a haven of sorts, how well do you suppose you can navigate yourselves without a guide?"

"I don't know," pondered Sarah; "I guess I can't."

"Though the morning began brightly, it is now too cloudy and foggy to utilize the sun as your guide. Your present situation is too large and too well-defended to transgress its boundaries successfully," said Paul with an emphatic, yet gentle suggestiveness.

"You only have two choices: you may trust the guide to navigate you through the course you have agreed to trek upon together..." Sarah kept her expression blank; "...or you may embrace desperation and flee through what appears to be an opening, tread upon the threshold you once crossed over hand-in-hand, be met by the storm you had already sensed was brewing, and accept an impending scourge without the support of the hand you once embraced."

Sarah and Jim exposed a mutual half-frown of guilt and confusion. "Either one of you, or the both of you, are free to leave whenever you desire, despite my wishes, but please recall that it was desire — no matter how misunderstood and misdirected — that compelled the two of you to have allowed me to marry you, to find your way to my abode, and to agree to walk *together* with me in my garden you yet know nothing of." The couple was taken aback a bit by Paul's frankness. "You may break your word and leave the garden, or you may keep your word; the gift is mine, but the choice is yours."

CHAPTER 35

The sunrise had, at first, blazed forth with crimson horns, only to have dense cloud-cover eventually play the cape of the matador. Paul paced forward in the morning mist that dangled below the stooping clouds. The storm between Jim and Sarah had already reached the condensation point, though Paul's soothing parlance had momentarily quelled the nearly torrential disaster. The young couple followed him while they engaged Paul in casual conversation which was speckled with observations and questions concerning the magnificent garden.

The garden was the result of terraced landscaping, precise irrigation, and continual upkeep that could not have been the sole labor of Paul, though Paul had explained that he was the sole owner of it. Jim and Sarah could only imagine what such an encapsulated world looked like in the fullest fructification of spring when the scents of sappy budding would fill the domain with angelic perfumes; but, the fall season had its own scents and its own colors that were in no way inferior to those of Spring, though they were in every way different. The smells were not thick with whiffs of flowers intermixed with the wet spring air that filled the nostrils; rather, the smells were thin and sharp, and they opened one's nostrils with an easily breathable bareness. The colors were not the bright, radiant hues of new life, but the darkening, deepening shades of languishing vigor. The landscape was marked by the fleeting essence of life that was covered with a foggy blanket. In Paul's garden, Autumn showed life wrapped in death and, with the promise of further nurturing, the promise of further life. Jim and Sarah sauntered with a mixture of sorrow and wonder as their collective hopes deteriorated in the midst of nature that was doing the same. Sarah could not help but think of her little flowerbox.

"The colors of the last drop of life are indeed beautiful, aren't they?" asked Paul.

"What?" asked Jim.

"I mean to say that is an amazing spectacle for nature to expose her deepest hues while she expires; people should observe and take note." Jim and Sarah striped their youthful brows before Paul's wintry countenance, and then they slipped each other glances of curiosity.

"Autumn instructs one to finish the ballad of life on a high note, for this season's touch swivels Vigor's diminution round about in a manner that unleashes the greatest blazes of life during the process of death. It is often Mortality's mark to reveal

its truest colors just prior to the scythe's chilling
caress, and it is ever humanity's test to reveal the
value of one's own substance in the midst of all that
is undesirable; for gold is not tempered in temperate
environments." Paul looked at Sarah and Jim — each
one had brandished a blade of cutting words against
the other, each one was wounded, both were on
the brink of despair, and both looked inwardly over
a chasm of failing, falling love that appeared to be
hurling toward oblivion.

The two noticed more statues. There were
various carvings that were cut into the rocky terrace-
walls, and there were various small statues that
stood on the lawns before them. The lawn statues
were spread far apart from each other, so that not
many could be seen at one time. The statues that
were carved into the walls of the terrace appeared to
look down upon the lower levels of the garden with a
lofty might of hardened mystery. The curiosity of Jim
and Sarah heightened with each statue they passed,
for the chisel had marked Paul's garden with figures
of animate life that looked frozen in walls of eroding
nature.

"Who terraced all this land?" asked Jim.

"My great-grandfather; this property has
been in my family for four generations; it is my
inheritance. Each successive owner has done his
part in augmenting the beauty of this place. My
great-grandfather terraced and carved statues into

the walls of the terraces. My grandfather irrigated and cultivated. My father tended and trained the vegetation. I have often looked at the faces of the older carvings on the terrace-walls... the statues from my great-grandfather's time. You would think that the stone faces would endure longer than they have endured...."

"What do you mean?" asked Jim. "I mean that the faces were much more distinct when I was a child, but time and the elements have surely touched them in a cruel way."

It was becoming obvious to the young couple that Paul was growing weary. "Are you OK?" asked Sarah.

Unintentionally ignoring her, Paul said, "You just need to listen."

"Listen to what?" asked Sarah, as she looked at her husband with concern for Paul.

"Listen to the story... the whole story. Too often, people do not listen to whole story, fall into despair, and stand alone, without valid excuse or true recourse," answered Paul, with heavy breath. "Children, let's, please, sit down on the bench over there, alright?"

CHAPTER 36

After walking nearly a block, the three sat down on a large, wooden bench that had been beaten by weather for many years. The fog was beginning to thin as the sun fought its way through the almost dominant clouds, and more of the garden appeared to emerge from beneath the misty cloak. Paul appeared more weak than tired, and he sat somewhat hunched forward with a dimly lit expression.

"Are you OK, Paul?" Jim asked.

"Yes... yes... I'm alright; thank you; it just feels like my sap is running dry. Such is life, or the end of it anyway; 'Autumn was there, stained with trodden grape....'"

"Huh?"

"...nothing... nothing...."

Jim and Sarah sat silently next to Paul. Paul smiled at the two of them with a gentleness that was more felt than discerned by the two. Paul's eyes projected all the radiance of a toddler eating ice cream, but his physical presence gave the impression of being antithetical to what animated it. Paul lifted his hand, as though it weighed 100 pounds, and pointed to a little bird that fluttered downward, with the falling leaves, and perched upon the rim of an ornate birdbath that stood about 15 feet away from the trio.

"It has never ceased to amaze me... when I consider the meticulous details that were put into such small creatures... their colors, their mannerisms, their voices.... I cannot imagine putting so much detail into something so small; and when I think about the size of my own frame compared to the breadth of the world and the vastness of the universe, it is incomprehensible for me to imagine why He would have put so much effort into making me. When I consider these things, to think that such tremendous effort was put into *everyone* and *everything* that was *ever* created astounds me, for even more effort must be required to join two individuals so that their individually minute details might become a collective detail. Oneness is often confused with singleness."

"What?"

"I mean that what was once plural becomes singular when a man and woman are joined in marriage, and this singularity replaces singleness."

CHAPTER 37

Jim, Sarah, and Paul watched the little bird that was perched on the rim of the birdbath. The pedestal on which the birdbath rested was a strange, stone sculpture of a goat that lay on his chest. The goat's body terminated into a fish's tail that then curled upward and over the center of the goat's body to support the basin.

As Jim and Sarah had taken their eyes off of the bird and had begun to view the sculpture, Jim mentioned, "You sure do collect interesting statues, Paul."

Paul smiled, paused for a moment, and responded, "I don't collect these statues; I sculpt them."

"You sculpt them?" asked Sarah.

"Yes. My great-grandfather sculpted the figures in the sides of the terraces, and I have sculpted the figures on the lawns." Then, changing the subject, Paul pointed towards the water of the birdbath and said, "Ancient stargazers used reflecting pools for observing the heavens." Jim and Sarah looked puzzled. "I don't want to bore you; let's keep walking;

I've had enough rest, and there is much for you to see." The three of them arose and began to saunter within the lush, declining, landscape.

As the three of them walked and talked together, Jim and Sarah noticed that there were other animal statues that stood in seemingly scattered locations. Lions and cows, sheep and wolves, predator and prey, speckled the strange grounds. Paul's garden was distinctly exotic, though the true essence of the garden's construction seemed to be veiled by a deeper logic than what met Jim and Sarah's eyes.

The three continued to saunter across the lawns lined by glistening, oozing, aromatic trees that added a delicious hint to the subtle breezes which sifted throughout the landscape. Though the flowers had withered, Sarah imagined how they must have looked only months before as they grew in patterns that seemed to paint some colorful picture that possessed some intricate intention. Trellises of varying sizes stood within the spacious property; they gave the appearance of something of a faded time, and it was apparent that the vines that slithered on top of them, hung beneath them, and coiled about their supports had been trained as such from a bygone era. Sarah was captivated by the fact that the girth of some of the vines was as thick as a python.

Paul noticed that both Jim and Sarah paid significant attention to the large vines on the old trellises; he began to walk towards one of the larger trellises. The young couple followed. Upon reaching the trained vines, Jim and Sarah beheld the slithering plants with wonderment and awe, since neither of them had ever before seen such large, manicured plants drooped so decoratively on such an imposing structure. The vines appeared as veins on rigid limbs.

In the midst of their interested gaping, Paul asked, "Have you ever heard anything concerning ancient blood covenants, you two?"

The couple was taken off-guard on account of Paul's seemingly grim and startling choice of conversation. "Ancient 'blood covenants?" asked Sarah.

"Yes; the blood covenant has quite an amazing and forgotten history," Paul said as he stood beneath a ceiling of vines; he inspected one vine carefully that was attached to a wooden support beneath the entrance to the trellis; he gave the impression of one petting a snake.

"What's the purpose of a 'blood covenant?'" asked Jim.

Paul's eyes sparked along with his sharp smile. "When we think of blood, we are often tempted to conjure gruesome images in our minds and to conceive of the morbid; however, such was not the case in the ancient east. In the direction of Antiquity's sunrise, blood stood for *life*, not death; it was understood that life was in blood."

"Life?" Jim asked with a confused expression.

"Yes, life.... When two parties would engage in a blood covenant, each party thought himself to take on a sort of double-life. In such a case, each covenanting party was willing to lay down his life for his friend, should the need arise, for in so doing, he would then save his own life." Sarah's brow produced folds; she asked,

"His own life? — how so?"

"If two covenanting parties shared in each other's blood, and blood indicated life, then each party shared in each other's life. As such, there were not two lives between the two covenant-makers; instead, there was one life between them. The fact that two people shared one life meant that one person saved his own life by giving his life for his counterpart."

Sarah began to smile, but then her smile evanesced as she continued to wrinkle her brow. She then asked, "If blood symbolized life, then why were the ancient people always killing animals for sacrifice and all that stuff?"

Paul kept his eyes on the vine before him. "Life was thought to be obtained by blood, for life was thought to be in the blood. It is thought, by more than one historian, that animal sacrifice preceded human consumption of animals — which would explain more of the very reason for animal sacrifices: the acquisition of blood meant the acquisition of life, even if such an acquisition cost some victim its life. The ancients, through animal sacrifice, were trying to acquire *life*, not death. The notion that life could be acquired through death placed death as more a means of an exchange than a punishment."

"Death was a 'means of exchange?'" asked Sarah.

"Yes; by the time the consumption of animals was prevalent, animal blood was often obtained in an effort to add life to the one who consumed it; however, the ancient Hebrews were quite distinct regarding this mindset, since they were disallowed from consuming any blood that had issued from any animate being. The only 'blood' they were allowed to consume was what they called 'blood of the grape,' i.e. wine. Ancient Jewish teachers used to say that 'wine sustains life,' for they regarded the 'blood of the grape' as *food* that 'gladdens the heart.' However, they also distinguished between moderate and excessive wine consumption, for they held that an excess of wine empties an individual, whereas the case was the opposite regarding moderate wine consumption...." Jim and Sarah shot each other quizzical expressions. "The relaxing, yet invigorating, effects of moderate wine consumption were intended to illustrate that *life* is in blood, and that the acquisition of blood is, ultimately, the acquisition of life itself. You can see why vines were such an important part of the ancient Hebrews' lives: blood indicated life, and wine was equivalent to blood; therefore, vines were viewed as stems of life, in a manner of speaking." Paul gently stroked the vine on which he had been concentrating; then, he looked at the two perplexed lovers. "Why do you think that wine was such an integral component of marriage?"

Jim and Sarah looked at each other, though neither of them knew what to say. "Marriage?" asked Sarah.

"Sure; it was understood that life was in the blood. In the same way, the ancient Hebrews understood that the soul was in the blood. The idea conveyed by the 'life' and the 'soul' being in blood forms the basis for our conceptions of what we call a 'soul-mate.'"

"How so?" asked Jim.

"If two blood-covenanting people take on the blood of each other, they then share one life, for they have taken on each other's life, correct?"

"OK," Jim replied.

"…and if the soul was understood, figuratively, to be in the blood, then we can understand how a husband and wife would have then been understood as 'soul-mates' who shared one life in two bodies. Anyway, those are the basics regarding our conceptions of soul-mates and such…. The whole idea is much older than many acknowledge. Do you understand how blood stood for life, how wine stood for blood, and therefore how a vine represented a source of life?"

Jim scratched his head and responded, "Sort of... yeah... I guess so." Paul's acute smile flashed at Jim and Sarah, but then he turned his concentration back on the vines before him as he spoke.

"In a similar way, the ancients often viewed a shared meal as a truce."

"A truce?" asked Sarah.

"Certainly; by the way, did the both of you enjoy breakfast this morning?"

CHAPTER 38

The young couple stood fixedly perplexed, as such a discussion was the furthest from what either of them had anticipated. Paul sauntered beneath the large, shady trellis as he inspected the coiling vines in a manner that intrigued both Jim and Sarah. There was a quiet beauty that shone from the slinky vines as Paul discussed little facets of their strange significance. However, Sarah found the serpentine appearance of the vines unsettling when she considered the concepts regarding the blood that Paul discussed. Jim found the entire turn of conversation a bit eerie, and he felt ill-equipped to do little else but listen.

Paul's aged hands were of proportions that suggested their strength in his youth, but his fingers were bent arthritically, and his movements seemed to cause him pain. He always stood perfectly erect and in a bow-chested manner, though it was evident that his physical prowess was long past. His silver hair sparkled, and his eyes flashed whenever he spoke, though the dark impressions beneath his eyes appeared to deepen by the minute; he continued: "The sharing of blood was taken as the knitting of natures, and such a knitting added life to the partakers."

"So," asked Sarah, "a meal between two parties was understood to indicate some sort of truce or something?"

"Sure," answered Paul.

Sarah gazed at the large trellis and the thick vines. She considered Paul's careful deliberation with them. Everything seemed strange, ancient, and vague. The more she examined the trellis, the more she thought of the delicious grape juice from breakfast. "Paul, that juice you gave us this morning was the best I have ever tasted. Where can I buy it?"

With his warm smile, Paul chuckled and said, "Well, if I sold it, then I guess you could buy it from me; but I don't buy it or sell it. I make my own grape juice, and I would be happy to give you as much as you like."

"Yeah?" said Sarah with her youthful glow.

"Of course, my dear; you're like family to me. I considered your grandfather like my own brother. Speaking of brothers and the fruit of the vine, a 'brother' made through blood-covenanting was often deemed closer than a brother by birth."

Battling to keep his patience long enough in order to get his wife to himself, Jim became accidentally short and asked, "Paul? — I don't mean to be rude or ungracious, but I'm curious to know why you ever wanted to meet with us in the first place. I mean, I'm having a lot of fun, and you're a really neat guy, but why should someone like you care about what we're doing, and why do you want to share all your stuff with us?"

Somewhat taken aback, Paul grinned and replied, "I always counsel young couples for quite a while before I am willing to marry them. However, since the two of you were planning a Las Vegas wedding, and since Sarah's grandfather disapproved of the idea so vehemently, he called upon me for a favor and asked if I would marry the two of you — with less than a week to spare.… As a favor to Sarah's grandfather, I married the two of you. However, I still feel responsible for sharing with you, especially after Sarah's grandfather passed away.

"Since over a couple of years have passed since your marriage, since I am not getting any younger, and since I am feeling my memories begin to slip away, I wanted, at least, to check on a couple I married, especially since you were the only couple I have ever married without prior counseling, and even more especially since you, Sarah, are the granddaughter of a man who was my best friend."

"Gotcha," acknowledged Jim.

"Thank you," responded Sarah.

"For what?" asked Paul.

"…for taking time to care about two insignificant people."

"No person is ever 'insignificant,' and our time together brings me joy." Paul smiled warmly again, though his teeth appeared as razors and his eyes had a piercing quality about them that could be intimidating at times. Paul rapidly switched subjects again: "As I was saying, the idea of sharing blood was attached to the concept of entwining natures. On a general scale, eating often presented a truce. However, in a specific sense, the nature of the entity whose blood was consumed was thought to be made part of the consumer. The exchange of blood would therefore combine the natures of the two, generally, and add the nature of the one being consumed to the consuming one, specifically."

"You mean, 'You are what you eat?'" chuckled Jim.

"Yes, that was the basic thought, Jim. When the blood of something was consumed, its nature was thought to be added to the one who consumed it; it is for this reason that the ancient Hebrews were not to eat rare meat or to drink blood."

"Well, wait a minute," pondered Sarah aloud; "If the ancient Hebrews weren't supposed to consume any blood, then wouldn't that make them the only people who didn't want to get more life?"

"Not exactly, but that is a good question. They *were* allowed to consume 'blood,' but not 'blood' that came from an animate being. The ancient Hebrews were allowed to drink the 'blood' of the grape. The Hebrew word 'grape' comes from the root *'to bind together'*; you can comprehend how grapes are so bound on the cluster and how the Hebrews understood people to be bound by the intentional sharing of blood. Furthermore, their word for 'tendril' comes from the root *'to interlace.'* Since the consumption of blood was thought to add life to the consumer, we can understand how the blood of the grape bound together those who shared it by interlacing their natures. However, it is important to remember that, when discussing blood, the ancient Hebrews usually described the human consumption of it as 'eating' and not 'drinking' in the Scriptures, similar to the reason for why the ancient Jewish teachers claimed that wine was to be considered as 'food,' even though it is liquid."

"So the rest of the world ate raw meat, or rare meat, or drank blood, or whatever, but the Jews didn't?" asked Sarah.

"The *Hebrews* did not; Abraham was a 'Hebrew' before there were any Israelites. Only a portion of the Israelites, after a set of straining circumstances, later became known as 'Jews.' Israelites began, technically, with a grandson of Abraham. A 'Hebrew' was someone of a particular faith, and therefore a particular way of life, not someone of a particular physical descent... that is why the people who believed, and believe, as Abraham believed are called 'the seed of Abraham,' i.e. 'Hebrews', even though

many such people are not Jewish. It is written: '...
when ye read ye may understand my knowledge in
the mystery...." Paul continued, "Abraham was not
Jewish, and Jewish people did not exist in the time
of Abraham. Jews confess, in the margins of some of
their Bibles, that they are unaware of the meaning of
the term 'Hebrew'; as such, they mistakenly mingled
the words 'Hebrew,' 'Israelite,' and 'Jew,' as did what
is called 'The Church.' The word 'Hebrew' comes
from a root that means 'to pass over,' and an idea
of 'impregnation,' along with a word that signifies
'produce of the ground,' comes from this same root
also. Since Abraham crossed, or passed over, the
Euphrates River because of his trust in God, he was
called a 'Hebrew' or one who 'passed over,' i.e. into
covenant with God. The name '*Euphrates*' means
'*fruitful,*' which is certainly what Abraham became
through his covenant with God.

"Though the words 'contract' and 'covenant'
are erroneously employed synonymously today, it
should be noted that a 'contract' is generally written,
but a covenant does not necessarily require written
documentation. Bloody sheets were once used as
'testimony'....

"Anyway, my original point is that the only
'blood' a Hebrew was allowed to consume was the
'blood' of the grape. Other ancient cultures shared
similar, but not congruent, concepts regarding
blood, and some of them even mingled blood with

wine; in time, many of those cultures used wine as a substitute for blood. The act of consuming blood carried with it the concept of melding natures. We can therefore see why the Hebrews were not to consume the blood of animate beings, even if they ate animals."

Jim and Sarah looked puzzled, and Sarah asked, "Why couldn't they consume animal blood? I'm sorry; I just don't get it."

"They were not to consume animal blood because, in so doing, they would have been believed to take on the nature of the animal they had eaten, metaphorically speaking," answered Paul.

"But I thought people wanted to get more life, and that's why they wanted blood," said Jim.

"You are correct; but the Hebrews acquired the blood they consumed from vines, not animals or people. They acquired blood through a source of life that, by the nature of such an acquisition, promoted further life — whereas the case is the opposite when acquiring blood from animals because it involves destruction, not productivity. In other words, they were to take on the nature of vegetation. A righteous man is like a tree planted besides streams of water. Through pruning, vines can become very fruitful and precious. Furthermore, vegetation, in general, exhibits a form of seasonal life and death; in this case, since leaves die each year, but are born again each year, vegetable life was used, quite often, to illustrate the resurrection... for nearly everyone has witnessed inanimate entities come back to life each year. Accordingly, the name 'Adam' is related to the word *red ground.*' Interestingly enough, the words 'Adam' and 'blood' are derived from the same root. It can be said that 'Adam' affords us a teaching of blood." Paul's breath became belabored.

"Hmph... 'teaching of blood, huh?" asked Jim.

"The 'blood' of the grape was consumed, and animal blood was used to illustrate atonement for sins."

"Excuse me, Paul; I have a question."

"Yes, Sarah?"

"What does this whole 'blood covenant' thing have to do with 'sin' and stuff? I thought we were talking about marriage."

"Good question, Sarah," Paul smiled. "You see, error or 'sin' was understood to usher death in like a stillbirth; that is, an ancient Hebrew wrote that 'sin gives birth to death'; therefore, the consumption of the fruit of the vine, the 'blood' of the grape, brought life to the consumer. Sins were forgiven through the shedding of blood that flowed through the veins of 'The True Vine.' The Hebrew word 'atonement' means, literally, a 'covering over.' Furthermore, this illustration is bound up in the idea of the ancient feasts of the Israelites, for their word for 'feast' or 'appointed time' comes from the root *'to betroth.'* Indeed, Jewish weddings have an 'unveiling,' where the groom peeks behind the veil of his bride; but, long before there were any Jews on the earth — during the days of Abraham — Eastern brides in and near the lands of Abraham's sojourn covered themselves in long, cloak-like veils before marriage; it was the bridegroom who unveiled her just prior to the consummation of their union. The Greek word for an 'unveiling' is often rendered in English 'revelation'; thus, '...the Spirit and the bride say, Come.' The first man's marriage became temporal, but the second Man's marriage will be eternal."

"So you're telling me," asked Sarah, "that those feasts had something to do with marriage?"

"Yes... marriage and conception... but that gets a little involved. For now, suffice it to say that when animals were eaten or offered in sacrifice, the Hebrews would slaughter them over a threshold."

"Why?" asked Jim.

"Their thresholds were formed like basins, and those basins would catch the blood of the sacrifice. They viewed a woman like a house, and the doorway to the house was the means by which life *passed over* as a result of marriage; we may understand why the terms 'Hebrew' and 'impregnation' come from the same source. By shedding blood, life was shed, and the ancients painted the doorway to their houses with life by slaughtering their animals over the threshold."

"—but you said that a 'Hebrew' was not defined by physical descent. Then why is a 'Hebrew' related to impregnation?" asked Sarah.

"— for the same reason that we often say that we 'conceive' of something when we mean that we are *thinking* of something. Remember, a Hebrew was a person of a particular belief, and this belief defined a Hebrew's ultimate lineage and unity. If someone is born a second time, the second birth can hardly be physical. One chooses to be a part of another's family through a blood covenant, but physical lineage is unchosen, and often uncherished. Accordingly, Diodorus' histories inform us that vines were said to have 'two births' in the ancient world: the first birth occurred when the plant first broke through the soil, and the second birth happened when the vine ripened its clusters.

"The first sacrificial altar was a threshold, and the first temple was a house. Viewing the human body as a temple caused sacrifices to be made upon altars, or tables, or, in this case, thresholds." Having noticed the perplexed expressions of Jim and Sarah, Paul added, "...but all that stuff gets a little complicated, and is more the substance of an academic study. Let's continue walking, shall we?" Paul suggested. "Hey... let me tell you about a 'paradise.'"

"Paradise?" asked Sarah.

"Not 'Paradise,' but 'a paradise'..." Paul replied. Jim and Sarah followed Paul more deeply into his garden, and they listened to his seemingly strange accounts of otherwise ignored history.

CHAPTER 39

Paul, Jim, and Sarah strolled over the spacious lawns of Paul's enclosure. Paul digressed again into stories of Sarah's grandfather. Some of Paul's remembrances brought Sarah into states of nostalgia, while other stories left the three of them laughing hysterically with joyful tears. Paul delighted in discussing Sarah's grandfather, and Sarah appreciated Paul greatly for it; by listening to him, she had begun to see a better-rounded picture of her grandfather, and her father, in a way she would not otherwise have known. From what Sarah could gather from fragments of Paul's stories, it seemed as though Paul and her grandfather had become friends near the time her grandfather became a widower; but each time one of Paul's oral histories began to lean towards sadness, he repeatedly found a way to direct his words towards sunshine. Dark clouds continued to pervade, and gray-blue hues painted the landscape.

Paul was always courteous, and he never left Jim out of the conversation. Paul was a good questioner, and his inquisitive nature made him adept at provoking people to divulge the beauties of their own histories and observations, of which Jim was stocked amply. Though Paul craved specificity and detail, he enjoyed a hearty laugh. He seemed pained in some unspoken way, though his sense of humor appeared in no way affected by it. The simple act of seeing the youthful beauty of his departed best-friend's granddaughter, and the observation of Jim's fondness for her, lit Paul's face into upturned crescents that facilitated further conversation, despite his obvious weariness. The three walked and talked for nearly half-an-hour, and Paul's endurance startled both Jim and Sarah.

□ □ □

"Let's walk over to that shed over there and sit down, shall we?" said Paul, as he pointed to what looked to be a tiny house.

"Sure," agreed Sarah. Jim followed in silent assent. The three of them walked towards a shed that was about the size of an apartment; it stood several hundred feet from their present location. The shed was situated delightfully beneath a large, shady tree. Paul's garden was enormous, and it was evident that a man of his age, if he were to tire as far out into his property as they had ventured, would find a resting-place, like this shed, of much need.

Paul's pace decreased within the two-block stretch that separated the three from the tiny semi-abode. However, he stoked a story from his flickering recollection that left a trail of laughter from yesteryear to their destination.

☐☐☐

"Sit here, you two," panted Paul, as he pointed towards a set of five wooden lawn-chairs that were situated in a semicircle in the shed's front lawn. Jim and Sarah sat down and relaxed while Paul busied himself within the little house; after a few moments, he emerged with two wooden cups that were filled with grape juice. Both Sarah and Jim perked up upon receiving the beverages, and they drank gratifyingly.

"I *love* this stuff, Paul."

"Thank you," he responded to Sarah.

"How did you learn to make this?" inquired Jim.

"My great-grandfather taught my grandfather, my grandfather taught my father, and my father taught me. If you like the juice, you'll love the wine." Jim and Sarah finished their juice speedily.

Seemingly out of nowhere, Paul began to say that, "Consuming the blood of the grape was thought to meld the nature of the vine to the nature of humanity. The ramifications by which humanity becomes fruitful and multiplies depends on the stem of life, that is, the True Vine."

Realizing that Paul was, once again, interested in strange conversation, Sarah swallowed, licked her lips and replied, "So, if I understand you, then you're saying that, by drinking wine, the ancient Hebrews understood themselves to be gaining life in a similar manner to how the rest of the world drank blood or ate raw or rare meat...."

"...and that by doing so," Jim added, they took on the nature of the vine itself... and since the vine stood for life, they acquired life and took on the very essence of life?"

"Yes; very good! Vines can grow quickly, but if left untrained and without pruning, they do not bear much fruit fit for consumption. So, you must distinguish between the various natures of different vines."

"Different vines?"

"Yes; vines that are trained and pruned are able to produce edible, pleasurable fruit. However, wild vines do not produce anything you would really want to eat, and they were sometimes used for fire-fuel. By pruning a vine, a husbandman stresses the plant so that it finds necessity to bear fruit in hopes of perpetuity. That is, if the vine feels no threat to its existence, it also feels no urge to reproduce. It is written, "I will greatly increase your conception and your childbearing...." Without a perceived threat, a vine will luxuriate itself relatively fruitlessly; consider, historically, how societies practiced child-sacrifice at the *height* of their populations…. Part of the definition of the name of the garden is 'luxury.' The threat of death produces fruit, and a cutting produces a duplicate. How astounding it is that a severance produces a duplicate when the lack of a duplicate produced a severance in the land of luxury! The first command given to humanity was to 'Be fruitful and multiply.' The first command given to nature was 'Let there be light,' and the Hebrews understood 'light' as life. The Hebrews held light, fire, and life in parallel. Consider how candles were once placed upon thresholds for a marriage, and consider the glint of a sword being wielded by a door-keeper. Pruning produces life, and cutting produces blood."

"Huh?"

"If I," Paul continued, "have a grapevine that I intend to use for wine production, I must continue to monitor its development and prune it accordingly. If I do not train up the vine in the way that it should go, it will cease producing the fruit it was intended to produce and it will subsequently grow towards disaster. Once this same vine becomes wild, nothing short of destruction is inevitable, for it will develop the power to kill trees or whatever else its fancy finds. Vines kill in the same manner as constrictor snakes. I knew of a man who let a wild vine take over his home until it imploded his house. Just put your finger on one of a vine's little tendrils and watch how quickly it will grow around your finger and begin

to squeeze. Since vines lack the initial hardiness
to stand upright on their own, their ascent is not
possible without something on which to cling. Wild
vines need other trees to hang themselves upon in
order to thrive, and at this point, the vine makes war
with the tree.”

“Makes war?” asked Jim.

“Yes; the war between vines and trees is a
struggle for height. The one who achieves the loftiest
height is the one who has access to the nourishment
of the light and of the rain, the food of life.”

“But if the vine needs the tree for support,
doesn’t the tree already have the access to the light
and the rain?” asked Jim.

“Yes, until a wild vine reaches the top of the
tree and begins to spread upon the canopy. Wild
vines can kill trees. In fact, the ancient Hebrews
called vines “trees” or “vine-trees,” though they, quite
often, paralleled vines to serpents as well. So, in their
nomenclature, such a tree could be a ‘serpent’ also.”

Taken by surprise once again on account
of Paul’s apparent, rapid change of subjects, Jim
responded, “Serpents, huh?”

“Of course... consider the vines on my trellises.
What do they look like to you?”

“...but,” asked Jim, “if wild vines were used for
fire fuel, you’d have to be really careful not to throw a
poisonous vine into a fire because burning something
poisonous would make toxic smoke that could really

mess you up if you got in your eyes or breathed it or something, right?"

"Certainly," affirmed Paul. "Just imagine the harm that would ensue if you actually ate it?"

"Ate it? Why would you do that?" asked Jim.

"Many people have died having consumed poisonous vegetation, though they, by ignorance, had no idea what they were getting into before they did so."

"Yeah, but," added Sarah, "if vines were called trees, and their fruit was like blood, then, could we say that eating from that fruit would be like melding one's nature to something deadly? I mean, if a vine was thought of as a snake also, then eating from a poisonous vine-tree would be like melding one's nature with the nature of a poisonous snake, right?"

CHAPTER 40

"Would you like more juice?" asked Paul. "I have much more than I can drink, and my workers don't come here on Saturdays."

"I was hoping you'd ask," responded Sarah shiningly. Though Paul's discussion of snakes did not exactly whet her appetite, Sarah did thoroughly enjoy the drink, and all of their walking had made her thirsty.

Paul lifted himself on his feet and remarked, "You know, Sarah, this is the happiest I've seen you since you came to my house last night. Isn't it nice to enjoy the simple things in life and to let stories unfold at a relaxed pace? I'll get you some more." Paul rose, turned, and walked back into the shed before Sarah could give him her cup.

Sarah and Jim both sat silently with their hands inside of their jacket pockets. The autumn air was wet and chilly, and the sun had become veiled behind the congregating clouds. Paul had diverted Sarah's attention away from the obvious pain she carried with her concerning Jim; however, Paul produced the opposite effect on Jim, since all Jim wanted to do was to get his wife alone so that they could work things out. Thus, when Paul was present, Sarah was at ease, but Jim was caught in patient tension.

After a moment, Paul returned with a large challis filled amply with the regal liquid. "Here you go," said Paul, as he handed the challis to Jim. Both Jim and Sarah looked confusedly at each other. Jim took a sip, and he then gave the cup to Sarah, who also drank.

"A prospective ancient eastern groom would share a cup of wine with a lady who had accepted him for marriage."

"What?"

"Nothing, Sarah; back to the grape and the threshold...." Sarah and Jim glanced at each other again. "In ancient times, a threshold was never to be trod underfoot; it was held to be sacred. We still retain remnants of such a practice when a bride is carried *over* the threshold by her husband just prior to the consummation of their marriage, their own passing-over.

"You see, a womb specifically and a woman generally were understood as a 'house.' Since the womb is where life is housed, and since woman is where the womb is housed, we can understand the metaphor. The Hebrews would say that God 'built houses' when they wanted to indicate that God blessed people with children. The first sacrificial altar was a threshold, and knowing that an altar was perceived to indicate femininity, then treading upon a threshold was as treading upon the basin, the entrance to house, the womb, the place where life was said to be 'built up.' Often, the foundations of antiquity's houses were at their entrances. To tread a threshold underfoot would have been among the most grievous insults one person could give another. Just imagine stepping on the foundation of a family!"

Pondering the foreign metaphors for a moment, Jim asked, "'...foundation of a family?' Does that have anything to do with blood that was contained in the threshold basins?"

"Yes, Jim; very good... for blood was poured in the threshold/basin, and blood was understood as life."

"I see," Jim responded.

"To tread upon the threshold was to crush life itself underfoot. The ancient Hebrews linked the heart of man to the womb of woman, for it is in the womb that life exists, and it is the heart which pumps the blood, that is, the life. A husband's love for his wife urges him to pass over her threshold so that a third can pass out of the man's house. Such imagery can even be found as late as the sixth book of Virgil's *Aneid*."

"You're talking about conception and birth, right?" asked Sarah.

"Certainly, for the only proper, acceptable, *suitable* context that a Hebrew would have understood copulation and impregnation was within the context of marriage." Paul looked at the couple speculatively. "Have either of you ever heard any part of the history of Abraham?"

"The Jewish guy you were talking about?" Jim responded.

"The *Hebrew* guy; remember that Abraham lived *before* there were any Jews," Paul reminded the two.

"Uhh... a little, I guess... I mean, apart from what you've already told us. I think I heard Gramps talking about him before."

Paul chuckled at Sarah's comment as he continued; "Abraham's name was not always 'Abraham.'"

"What was it before?" asked Sarah.

"Abram."

"Sound's almost the same to me," said Jim.

"A wild vine and a trained vine are both vines. Do either of you know what a difference between the two is?"

"A trained vine produces *suitable* fruit."

"Very good, Sarah... very good.... Yes, a trained vine produces *suitable* fruit. But how is the vine trained?"

"On a stake or tree, right?"

"Right... on a stake or on a tree... and once a trained vine hangs on the stake, he must be pierced in order to bear fruit, for all pruning requires the knife. The ancient Hebrews paralleled such piercing or pruning to circumcision.”

"—like how men are circumcised?” asked Jim.

“Exactly; it is quite easy to discern why the ancients sometimes likened anatomical masculinity to a vine and its clusters.”

Jim thought for a moment and then asked, “How does this relate to Abraham or Abram or whatever his name was?”

“If I do not prune a vine, and I let it become wild, then what will that wild vine do?”

“It’ll climb trees?”

“Correct. In fact, by climbing trees, wild vines war with trees, right?”

“Right,” Jim responded.

“Then how does a wild vine defeat a tree?”

“It has to reach the top of the tree and spread so that it gets the water and light before the tree does, right?”

“Right. So the battle is for height?”

“Yes.”

“The name ‘Abram’ means ‘Father of Height.’ Abram’s possessions and company spread quite broadly during his days on the earth. Abram was both very wealthy and valiant in war, and he had influence over a large number of people; but, he lacked one thing.”

“What’s that?” asked Sarah.

“He had no child.”

"Hah! You mean he had no *fruit*. You mean that, since the fruit of the vine is like blood, which is like life, then the 'Father of Height' had no life?"

"Well, almost; he had no *perpetuity*. He himself was magnified luxuriantly, but he had no sustentation or perpetuity, no lineage to pass on, no heir to his height."

Sarah pondered the conversation for a moment, but then added, "But wild vines perpetuate. Wild vines have seed. If wild vines didn't have seed, there would only be one wild vine."

"Very good," said Paul.

"Well then how does Abraham compare to a wild vine?"

"He does not."

"But you just said that Abraham was like a wild vine."

"I did not; I said that Abram, not *Abraham*, was like a wild vine."

"But wild vines and trained vines are both vines."

"True; and they can be the exact same vine, though the distinction between them depends on the stage of development under discussion — just as Abram and Abraham describe one man; this man's respective names defined the developing states of his life."

"How so?"

"Abram was the 'Father of Height,' like a wild

vine. However, as Sarah pointed out, wild vines do have seed and Abram had no 'seed'; but, I ask you, is the fruit of a tree for the tree itself, or for others?"

Thinking to herself for a moment, Sarah responded, "The fruit of a tree is for others; trees can't eat their own fruit."

"Wonderful, Sarah, wonderful! Wild vines do have seed, but their seed is not suitable for eating or for any good wine… their wood is, mostly, useless, and the vine cannot even stand upright on its own until much time has elapsed; this is the reason that wild vines need trees and trained vines need stakes or trees. A vine's branches cannot exist without the vine, and a vine cannot stand without the support of a tree, at first. So, the tree hosts the vine-tree, and the vine-tree hosts its own branches; the branches of a wild vine produce fruit, but the fruit is not fit for others. However, only a trained vine —"

"— You mean a 'circumcised' vine," added Jim.

"— Yes! A circumcised vine is what bears fruit fit for others, and all pruning requires the knife; after the knife pierces, the fruit may come forth abundantly. Knowing the 'blood' of the grape was understood as life, and that piercing a vine produces an abundance of fruit, then you can see how those who receive the abundance have life and have it more abundantly. Hence, God, in His Divine Grace, changed Abram's name to Abraham because 'Abraham' means 'Father of Multitudes,' in the same manner that, even though a wild vine and a trained vine are both vines, only a trained vine produces fruit suitable for others. Similarly, circumcision facilitates the process of man's fruitfulness, and pruning allows a vine to produce more abundantly for others."

"Wait. Say that again," Jim requested.

"All pruning requires the literal reduction of the vine; the vine is humbled and taught to be obedient to the stake; it is pierced, and the abundance flows; those who receive the abundance have life, and they have life more abundantly. Wild vines exalt themselves to apparently triumphant heights, but in their self-magnification, they produce little that is useful. Trained vines accept humility, and are not only useful, but valuable. Wild vines are often a detriment, but trained vines are always a joy."

"In the same way that wine produces joy?" asked Jim.

"Calm down, Jim," chuckled Paul. "Wine is used in joyous occasions, but a superabundance of wine produces sorrow; keep that in mind." Then, with his apparent randomness, Paul said, "God refers to Himself as a Husband Who has been betrayed by His wife in the third chapter of the Book of Jeremiah, and the subject of a Husband's indignant decision to divorce is discussed. In a similar way, Adam and his wife, who was named 'Eve,' that is 'Life,' *after* she fell into transgression, were driven from the garden. There are two words that are used to describe the

expulsion of humanity from Eden in the third chapter
of the Book of Genesis, and both words can also mean
'divorce' in Hebrew; this agrees with the fact that the
name 'Eden' comes from the same root as a word for
anatomical femininity that is fruitfully viable."

"Like a 'house' or a 'womb?'

"Right, Sarah; like a womb... and since we
know that the entrance to the house was understood
as an altar, and the first sacrificial altar was a
threshold, and since a threshold was to be filled
with life, we can understand part of the nature of a
covenant's injury when the threshold is tread under
foot.

"A vine must be pruned in order to be fruitful,
and an unpruned vine was called an 'uncircumcised'
vine by the ancient Hebrews. In the nineteenth
chapter of Leviticus, that which is described as
'forbidden' is the same word as 'uncircumcised.'"

Sarah thought for a second, but then Jim
replied, "So you're saying that an uncircumcised vine
is the same as a forbidden tree?"

CHAPTER 41

A cool breeze blew more expiring leaves from the trees. A vine cast its fruit. The crispness of the air caused the juice that the three drank to be even more desirable. The thought of imbibing life had relaxed Sarah and had fascinated Jim, who was beginning to become more patient after Paul's discussion of history's first divorce. However, the thought of drinking blood that came from plants that resembled serpents left Sarah's imagination in an undesirable state. The sky grew darker as clouds continued to climb over the tree-tops. Jim's attention had been captured, and he began to question Paul: "So let me get this straight; blood indicated life, and grapes were understood to hold blood. Vines were also called 'trees'; and since vines appear to look like snakes, then snakes were linked to blood and to trees?"

"Sort of, Jim…. You must distinguish between trained vines and wild vines."

"So wild vines are the ones that grow on trees — and don't produce fruit you want to eat, and trained vines are the ones that grow on trellises or stakes — that do produce fruit you want to eat?"

"Yes, that is basically correct; some gardeners used living trees as trellises or stakes, and this was common in both the ancient East and in our own country. In fact, the situation of a vine attached to a tree was called a 'wedding' from before the earliest historical documents, for the two entities became one in this manner; but, let us simplify. A man and wife partake of each other's wine and become unified."

"You mean, a man and wife partake of each other's blood?" asked Jim.

"Now you can see part of the reason why virginity prior to marriage was such a big deal to the ancient Hebrews. When the man opened the door to his house, the threshold was to be filled with life."

"You mean filled with blood?" asked Sarah.

"Yes, which helps us understand the importance of a pure, virgin bride — not that the man had any less responsibility than his wife in terms of being a virgin prior to their marriage also. I am merely using figures to show how the concept and the anatomy of the matter are unified, that's all."

Jim looked at his lovely wife, and then he turned his gaze to the landscape before him.   Sarah questioned Paul more and more about the imagery he described. While Paul and Sarah talked, Jim proceeded to look at the door to Paul's shed, and he considered the grape juice that was kept inside of it.

Accidentally, Jim interrupted the discussion of Paul and Sarah and asked, "If I understand what you are saying about wine, blood, houses, and thresholds as all being related to marriage, then what we call a marriage 'contract' was not the original design, was it?"

Both Sarah and Paul sat up with surprised expressions. After a moment, Paul said, "You have understood beautifully, because marriage was, originally, a *covenant*, not merely a contract. Contracts involve *written* legalities apart from the heart, whereas covenants involve the heart and are not necessarily accompanied by written documentation. Now, we may understand more of why the Hebrews' concept of laws being written upon the heart, and not on stone or parchment or clay or paper, indicated something covenantal."

"Wait a minute..." said Sarah; "...when you say, 'heart,' you're indicating love?"

"Yes."

"Then why would contracts ever have become part of the marital covenant?"

Paul frowned and said, "Since many young couples today reduce marriage to a mere contractually-binding aim towards what they think is happiness, it is no wonder why so many marriages break apart so quickly... it is like a man taking a bunch of oranges and agreeing with his fiancé to be bound to him for a lifetime of eating apples, but then the two becoming upset when they consistently bite into oranges." Jim and Sarah looked at Paul with curiosity. "Think about it; it's like a man unwittingly entering into a covenant with his wife along the guidelines of a mere contract; it's impossible."

"How so?" asked Jim.

"Covenants, like the blood covenant we are discussing —"

"— You mean marriage?" asked Sarah.

"Yes; covenants, like marriage — which are, or are supposed to be, blood covenants — are intended for the duration of a pair's *life*, hence the *blood*. Mere contracts are unions that exist only as a set of terms that are agreed upon. If I enter into a contractual agreement with a business partner, I am not of one body, mind, or spirit with her; I am only a partner with her along the guidelines of our business together. Under a contract, our business becomes strictly legal and does not reflect either of our hearts. Contracts usually deal in the realm of services rendered; should we apply contracts to marriage instead of recognizing the original covenant that marriage was intended to be, we reduce marriage to little more than an escort service. As escorts come and go, so we have modern marriage and its indifference towards the fruit it bruises."

CHAPTER 42

The three sat quietly. The sky's thin light decreased. The air seemed wetter. A warm gust shot through the chilly air and upon the three as they reclined beneath the large tree that overshadowed Paul's shed. Paul broke the silence and said, "Let's consider again the concept of consuming blood, that is, of mingling two natures into one. Consuming 'blood' was viewed figuratively as taking on the nature of the thing from which that 'blood' issued; such a nature would be obtained through choice."

"Then," said Sarah, "our choices are not far from our natures, and our natures are influenced by what we ingest."

"Yes! Exactly! — but consider: have you ever made poor choices?" asked Paul.

"Sure, who hasn't?" Sarah answered.

"Did you reap the detriments of such choices?"

"Yeah," regretted Sarah.

"Did such detriments affect your emotions?" asked Paul.

"Sure."

"Did such emotions affect your personality?"

"Yes."

"Then your choices affected your personality?"

"Yeah."

"...and your personality reflects your nature?"

"Ok."

"...and ingesting something's essence is likened to taking on that something's nature?"

"Yep."

"So, wouldn't your personality reflect those things which you have put into your own being?"

"I guess so."

"Then, my dear, whatever you accept and allow into your being causes your nature to attach itself to your allowances. There was a saying in the ancient east: 'Does not the ear taste words like the palate tastes food?'"

Sarah pondered the point for a moment, looked at her husband, then looked back at Paul. "Then words are like 'food'?"

"Yes, for, in ancient Hebrew, a word for 'tree' is spelled the same as a word for 'counsel.' The ancient Hebrews had another proverb: 'Death and life are in the power of the tongue, and those who love it will eat its fruit.' Jim raised his eyebrows. Paul continued; "They had another saying: 'How sweet are Thy words unto my taste! Yea, sweeter than honey to my mouth!'

"So good words are like good food?"

"Yes, Sarah," said Paul.

"Then bad words are like bad food?" asked Jim.

"Certainly."

"So words are like food and snakes are like vines?" asked Sarah.

"Yes."

"So a poisonous vine would produce poison just like a venomous snake would produce venom?" asked Jim.

"Uh-huh."

"And poisonous snakes produce death just like poisonous vines produce death," Sarah murmured.

"...Sure, just as venomous words produce death. How did it feel to you the last time you were cut by someone's words? Did it affect your emotions? Did your emotions affect your personality? Did your personality affect your nature? So, harkening to someone's words was once understood as 'eating' someone's words; if words were on a scroll, then the reader 'ate' the scroll; if words were spoken, then the ear 'tasted' such words.

"Now, I ask you, how have your words affected others? — you don't have to answer; the question is rhetorical. I just want you two happily married people to consider what manner of words you plant into each other's ears, how those words grow, and what is subsequently produced. A wild vine that threatens a tree can be humbled to produce fruit or can be cut down and thrown into the fire. Improper thoughts, if caught in time, can be subdued.

"Poorly-chosen words, even though they cling to the reality of another's nature, can be cut down through loving forgiveness and thrown into the fires of oblivion, should one's heart burn enough for a loved one."

Jim considered the conversation's direction, and then asked, "So, not only do even our flippant words affect others deeply, but what we put into our minds also, ultimately, affects others as well, right?"

Paul leaned forward in his chair and asked, "Let's consider what you've just deduced and follow it for a while, shall we?"

Jim glanced at his wife, then back at Paul and reluctantly said, "OK."

"Well then, consider the fact that good has always been good and evil has always been evil. The fact that such opposing traits, like good and evil, have taken on various forms in order to fit themselves to the time and location of people does not change the very essence of good or of evil. Good is, and always has been, good. Evil is, and always has been, evil. Therefore, it is evident that if you disregard whatever means by which good or evil comes, the root of their natures can be observed easily. Let us consider the 'means' to be what is incorrectly called 'technology.' If you love your wife, Jim, would you be unfaithful to her?"

"No... of course not!" exclaimed Jim, as Sarah fixed her eyes on him.

"If you love your husband Sarah, would you be unfaithful to him?"

Sarah turned her eyes from her husband and replied with a soft, "No."

"Let us consider that the language people use commonly today often comes from various forms of electronic media. We have already understood that words are like food. We have also understood how 'eating' is similar to making 'food' part of oneself. Let us say that, oh... I don't know... a husband and wife sat down and watched programs where the private 'intimacy' of others was depicted outright; is such a program healthy to ingest?"

With an agitated and somewhat offended tone, Jim objected by saying, "Well, it's not like the viewer is the one actually doing it."

"Do you pay a certain bill so that you can watch such depictions?" asked Paul.

"Well sure; who doesn't?" Jim defended.

"...and good and evil have been the same from time immemorial, despite whatever forms they take?"

"Yeah. So what?"

"...and if we eliminate the means by which various depictions are transmitted, we will then perceive the essence of what is being done?"

"OK; I guess so."

"Then, without such 'technological' means, or rather, before such technological means, in order for one to watch bedroom intimacy in the manner that is commonly done on various programs, one would have to engage in such acts himself or pay others to allow him to watch what others do, right?"

"Yeah... OK."

"If you pay a certain bill so that you can watch such depictions, then you are paying for a situation that is available through a certain means. You have already agreed that by eliminating the means, in this case, the 'technology,' you can perceive the true essence of the matter. Therefore, you are paying to be part of someone else's 'intimacy'... if that's what you want to call it, for such 'actors' or models only do such things on camera for money. Without the technological means under discussion, the only way people could ever view such things is either by voyeurism or through some means of prostitution; but the fact that such acts are now accomplished through a screen, people somehow consider those acts to be separate from what is being depicted and they proclaim such depictions to be acceptable — even laudable! — for the entertainment of the masses and for the collective enjoyment of the family, who often sit with each other and partake of such depictions. Yet, as the popularity of such depictions has increased, so has the number of divorces. I often wonder if there is a correlation....

"It has always amazed me to find a wife so broken and distraught over the fact that her husband has been unfaithful to her, yet both the man and

his wife spent years together paying to watch others
do the very thing that has wrongfully happened to
her. So long as she paid to watch others' misconduct
and suffering, be it fictional or factual, all was
well; however, once the very same misconduct and
suffering was applied to her personally, she became
indignant. The woman who is so distressed because
her husband has acted out the very thing she craved
to watch might benefit if she stops and asks herself
whether or not it matters if such depictions are called
'real' or 'make-believe.'"

"Why?" asked Sarah.

"Pretended affection for money once had an
uglier name than 'acting.' Such depictions only
occur because so many pay to watch them. If no
one paid to watch, there would be no market for
such depictions. If there were no market for such
depictions, such things would cease to be. Can a
man allow such a growth to penetrate his household
and not think that an infection of this manner will
affect his children, his wife, and himself? Won't his
children condone, and even imitate, the very things
their own bread-winner and guardian allows? — will
not their natures become like what their bread-winner
feeds them?"

Jim grew cross and replied, "Whoa... wait a
minute; it's not like we look at X-rated things, Paul."

"'X-rated' according to what standard? The
X-rating of yesteryear is the 'R' of today. The 'R' of

today will be the 'PG 13' of tomorrow, and so on,
until the rating ceases to be important at all. Basic
children's programming today was once the extreme,
underground taboo of yesteryear that was acted out
in pagan debauch. Surely you have noticed this
downward trend, and surely the 'R' that you speak of
would look exactly the same to you as it would if you
looked through someone else's bedroom window. The
only difference is that if one looked through another
couple's window, the only people who would be
affected would be those engaged in the act and those
who observed the act. However, since the invention of
the electronic screen, millions of people, particularly
children, can now be affected all at once. Which one
is worse?

"Accordingly, various terms have crept into
common language that reflect the fruit of such
choices; such choices affect people's natures;
such natures are reflected and passed on from
generation to generation, and we may comprehend a
degeneration that is not perceived until it is too late.
A rating-system is like a water-filter; the fact that the
filter is needed shows that the stream itself is dirty."
Paul seemed to change subjects yet again by asking,
"Do either of you think that worshipping a bronze
statue of a bull sounds silly?"

Somewhat surprised, Jim responded, "Of
course."

"Can you imagine bowing to a statue and giving it food for an hour per day, seven days per week?"

"Of course not," answered Sarah with a slight giggle.

"I always found it odd that most people wouldn't spend seven hours per week giving food to a statue, but the same are happy to give over 20 hours per week of their time, and more than their tithe's worth of money, to a talking light-bulb. One might not take His Name in vain, yet that same one enjoys programs where others take His Name in vain. How quick one can be to allow a little bad for the sake of some perceived good (!), for it was the Tree of the Knowledge of Good *and* Evil... it was the *admixture* that ruined the whole."

"Admixture?" questioned Jim.

"Is a glass that is nine parts water and one part putrescence drinkable? Is a show that is nine parts righteous and one part wicked a 'good' show? The forbidden tree was both 'good' and 'evil'; the antithetical admixture ruins the whole. Those things that you accept and allow into your being cause your nature to attach itself to your allowances. Choices cling to, and shape, the reality of one's nature. Consider what you allow into your being and who such choices ultimately affect.

"If something can be thought, it can be said; and if something can be said, it is that much closer to being done. Therefore, we may reflect again how our choices are not far from our natures, and our natures are influenced by what we ingest.

"A physical eye that is placed ahead of eternal sight does not lead to anything worthwhile; with respect to marriage, the best it can point towards is but a contract... and since contracts do not involve the heart, just as physical sight does not involve the heart, you can understand why contracts are just as cold as the eventual emotions that were founded upon mere physicality."

"How amazing it is that one could walk into a group of 'believers,' blaspheme the Almighty, commit every form of lewdness and destruction, and walk out of that group with a family of friends who shower the offender with pity... yet one could walk into the same group of 'believers,' speak against their favorite programs, and walk out of that group with life-long enemies!"

▫▫▫

After an awkward silence, Paul attempted to stand, but he was only able to raise himself upon his second attempt. Gusts of cool air blew against blasts of hot air. The birds twittered and flew in a fleeing manner. The distant trees appeared to shiver as their leaves fluttered from them. The air hissed along the tops of the trees, and the clouds moved like rapidly rising smoke. Several flashes reflected from Paul's eyes as lighting cut the sky above them. Thunder rolled distantly like a threatening growl.

"I don't think we'll be going anywhere for a while. Come children; let's get into the shed." Paul sauntered under a large awning, through the doorway, and into the small, dark edifice.

CHAPTER 43

Jim and Sarah followed Paul into the structure that resembled a tiny house. An old, shriveled wineskin hung on the doorknob. The early afternoon had grown as dark as dusk. The blackening clouds no longer exuded weariness; rather a quiet fear overshadowed the landscape.

Once inside the shed, Sarah and Jim noticed that there were two rickety couches that formed an "L" in a corner of the small house. They sat down and dust floated upward. Paul stood next to a raw-wood shelf and a rustic countertop. What little space was left inside the shed was lined with barrels of wine and grape juice. A couple of small cabinets, stocked with a few cups and glasses, projected from one wall. The little abode was equipped with clean, running water, and Paul stood next to the sink and washed the cups from which he, Jim, and Sarah had recently finished drinking.

Rain drops began to sprinkle the grounds outside the shed. Jim and Sarah sat quietly on the couches. Paul stood before the open door and gazed upon what would soon become a tempest. Jim and Sarah were convinced that, by running, they could

make it back to Paul's house before the storm hit;
but, they knew that Paul was unable to do so, and so
they continued to sit patiently, yet uncomfortably.
Distant thunder continued to approach the shed.
The clouds spread like a parasol and pressed a deep,
sanguinolent shade upon the sapid garden. Flashing
intervals of frightening luminescence sliced through
the dim heavens upon the darkening landscape like a
shining sword of heavenly fire. The thunder bellowed
like an angry voice in preparation to unleash a torrent
of royal fury.

With his usual sangfroid, Paul remarked,
"It has always amazed me that the very storm that
ravages a landscape can also purify the air," as he
continued to stand before the open doorway and as he
looked outward into what appeared to be an evening
sky, even though it was only early afternoon. Paul
held his cup in equanimity and silence as he stared
into the crimsoning heavens; he then pondered his
sanguine reflection in his cup. "The ancient eastern
thresholds were also called 'basins' and they were
held in the same regard as cups and bowls. In fact,
the Hebrew word *'beh'-ten'* describes a 'bowl,' a 'belly,'
and a 'womb'; it is related to a Hebrew word for
'threshold" — *'saph'* — by the fact that a 'saph' was a
basin.   Like I said before, when an animal was to be
sacrificed ritually, or merely eaten for supper, it was
usually killed at the entrance of the house and over
the threshold, the basin."

"Well isn't that kind of morbid? I mean, if both a house and a threshold represent a woman, why would they kill something in front of a house and over a threshold?" asked Jim. Lightning severed the sky with a brilliance that caused the two to blink.

"Remember, Jim, blood was understood as life..." A blast of thunder ripped through the ears of the three and pounded their chests. Paul continued, "...blood was life to the ancient easterners; they were painting the entrance to their dwellings with life. That death was the means to do so was indicative of human failure, and the ritualistic slaughter of animals was intended to serve as the reminder of human short-comings. The confidence of such a ritual was never meant to be in the death of the animal, but in the life that painted the entrance to the home."

"So why or how did a house become understood as a woman?" asked Sarah.

"I know I have mentioned it before, but I did not ask... Have you two ever read the Garden of Eden narrative?" Jim shook his head negatively.
Sarah responded, "No; I wasn't brought up with all that stuff. Gramps used to tell me tid-bits here and there, but my dad never believed all that stuff."
"He did before your mother died," said Paul in a low, lamenting manner.
"What?"

"Nothing... anyway, consider the fact that, in ancient times, babies were not born in hospitals, but in houses. In the story of Eden, the Hebrew Text states that the Lord God 'built' up the side, or rib, of the man into a woman. God 'built' her, as a carpenter would build a house. The man was to cross the woman's threshold, dwell in her, and, eventually, a third member of their family was to pass over the threshold in the opposite direction and out of the house the man had entered." Thunder cracked overhead, and Sarah flinched.

"So, concerning the creation of woman, the Story explains..." — thunder blasted loudly and both Jim and Sarah recoiled — "...the origins of marriage?" asked Sarah, as she squirmed a little in her seat. Paul's eyes seemed to grow darker, and his face took on a rather drained, ashen appearance. Paul breathed heavily. "Certainly... yes; as I said, the customs we are discussing date as far back as marriage itself," said Paul, in a voice of decreasing vigor.

"Even as far back as Eden?" asked Jim.

"Even as far back as Eden.... It is partially for this reason that a 'fruitful womb' shares the same root as the word 'Eden' in Hebrew; so, when Abraham's wife pondered the idea of returning to a youthful enough physical state in order to produce a child, she referred to such a state with a word that is connected to the name 'Eden.'"

"Well then what's the deal with the whole 'rib' thing," asked Jim.

Paul smiled, though his posture had become uncharacteristically slack so that his bow-chested manner had become almost concave. Nevertheless, he continued by stating, "The side that was 'built' up into a woman is understood as a rib because the chief function of the ribcage is to guard the heart. That the man's rib was removed in order to build his house is a literary method of stating that man's heart was exposed to woman, not that males have one less rib than females!" The three of them laughed heartily. "Man was to love woman, enter into his house, and from there, have his family built. After stepping over the threshold, so as never to tread life underfoot, man entered into a blood covenant with his wife whereby the two mingled their natures in an effort to form one new nature. That is, one new nature was formed from the two through a covenant of life, for life, that produced life. Man's heart was exposed... man's heart was circumcised... 'This is a great mystery, but I speak concerning....'"

Sarah pondered the topic at hand momentarily; then she asked, "You alluded to the fact that what is called an 'uncircumcised vine' is the same as a 'forbidden tree,' and that a vine was compared to a snake, right?"

"I'll answer your question this way: The first command given to humanity was to 'be fruitful';

despite English translations, the Hebrew Text says nothing about any 'fruit' that Adam and his wife were to *avoid*. As far as the forbidden tree... the situation of a vine on a tree was called a 'wedding.' Vines were paralleled to snakes, and an untamed, uncircumcised vine was understood as a forbidden tree. The Hebrews called wine that was undiluted with water 'fruit of the tree'; they called properly diluted, and therefore permissibly drinkable wine, 'fruit of the vine.' The Hebrew word for 'grape cluster' comes from the root 'to suffer abortion.'"

"Huh?"

"In what we now call the first three chapters of the Hebrew Text, the only time God mentioned 'fruit' with regard to humanity was in the case of the so-called 'fruit' they *were to produce* with their bodies, and the fruit that they *could* eat; He said nothing regarding 'fruit' that they *could not* eat. Regardless of English translations, the first one to bring up forbidden 'fruit' was not God, nor Adam, nor Satan, but the woman."

The rain began to pour heavily from the sky onto the moribund grounds. Paul allowed the door to hang open, since the large awning above it kept the inside of the shed dry despite the weighty condensation. The brown grass glistened beneath the driving tempest. No animal voices could be heard. No birds could be seen flying. The falling rain whispered, "Shhhhhhhhhhh...."

CHAPTER 44

The sky continued to blacken. The rain surged. The lightning stabbed its way through the clouds. The door to the shed remained open. Paul looked weary; he then spoke with a strained voice, as though it required great effort for him to articulate. "When the man's 'side' was opened, so as to expose his heart to his wife, he was not repaired with a replacement rib; rather, He 'closed' up the place with flesh, not bone."

"OK... so what's this part supposed to mean?" asked Jim. Paul's smile seemed to be blended with a grimace. Paul closed the door, and the shed's interior grew exceedingly dark. The only light source within the shed, at this point, was the stream of dim rays that crept in from the two windows on either side of the door. Paul made his way towards the couches, and a spark of lightning flashed through the window and reflected in his glistening eyes and widening, slicing smile.

"We use the expression 'tender-hearted' to describe affection. When it is stated that the man's side was 'closed' with flesh, it is the same word used for describing a door that is 'closed.' Adam's heart was softened towards his wife; his love was exposed to her.

"The Hebrew word for 'flesh' is also the word for 'people' — as we read in the 21st chapter of Ezekiel; this Hebrew word for 'flesh' is spelled the same as the word for 'good news,' 'gospel'... that is, Adam's heart was circumcised, and the man and woman became one *person*; the two became one gospel, one proclamation of good news! — they were married, like the True Vine on a tree.... As I said before, if two covenanting parties shared in each other's blood, and blood indicated life, then each party shared in each other's life. There were not two lives between the two covenant-makers; there was one life between them; they were one person. The fact that two bodies shared one life meant that one person saved his own life by giving his life for his counterpart. Again, 'This is a great mystery, but I speak concerning....'" Paul sat amidst the young couple. After he sat, Paul leaned back into the couch and exhaled heavily; his eyelids began to droop. Jim sat silently as he watched the storm.

Sarah continued to sit and to ponder Paul's words. "The man's heart was exposed to the woman, and you said earlier that the man's heart was paralleled to the woman's womb in ancient times, right?"

"Very good, my dear... very good... You're getting the picture. Your grandfather always told me what a sharp cookie you were..." said Paul in a brittle voice. He leaned back into the couch with half-opened eyes.

"Paul, are you OK?" asked Sarah.

Paul inhaled deeply and with difficulty, held his breath, then exhaled heavily and with ease. "Yes, my dear... yes, you understand well... yes, I'm fine... wonderful... you seem to have another question. What is your question?"

With a raised eyebrow, Sarah glanced at Jim, who looked back at her uneasily, and the two observed Paul with concern. "Paul? Are you sure you're —"

"— I'm fine; you have come very far during your short journey; ask while there is time."

"Time for what?" asked Sarah.

"Ask, and I will answer as best I can. The door is open. Ask."

Sara looked at Paul with resignation, but she did what he told her to do; "We've talked about blood being in the doorway; but what blood did the woman partake of?"

Paul sat back up, turned to Sarah and answered with surprisingly renewed vigor (but with a softening, weakening voice), "The woman shared the wine of grapes with her husband prior to the consummation of their marriage; the husband covered his vessel with the wine of her virginity; the man's vessel functions in this manner by being filled with blood or 'life'; in this sense, there is an exchange of blood that is intended to produce more life. However, since the only blood that is actually spilled belongs to the woman, then, in that sense, it is the man who partakes of the blood, and it is the woman who becomes part of the man; it is partially for this reason that the Hebrew Scriptures refer to a woman's threshold as the a 'man's nakedness' in the twentieth chapter of the Book of Leviticus. However, let us bear in mind that there is a natural co-dependence between the man and the woman, for, in their union —" lightning lit the room beyond the capability of any house-lamp, "— the wine of virginity paints masculinity with life, and masculinity paints femininity with life, though not with blood, but through his means that is filled with blood, for the man's vessel is like a branch." Thunder tore through the churning robe of clouds.

"So a man's 'nakedness' means his wife's anatomy?" asked Sarah.

"Yes," said Paul. "The twentieth chapter of Leviticus calls a man's wife 'his nakedness'; the twenty-seventh chapter of the Book of Deuteronomy and the twenty-second chapter of the Book of Ezekiel speak in a similar fashion. How else do you think that, regarding the True Vine, His 'bride' is also His 'body'? — would this not explain more of why the ancient Hebrews spelled *body*, *flesh*, and *good news* the same way?"

"What?" Sarah shot Paul a confused glance, but then asked, "If the name 'Eden' comes from the same root as female anatomy —"

"—anatomy *that is capable of producing fruit*," Paul added, with a raised index finger.

"...then wouldn't the name 'Eden' refer to 'man's nakedness' as well?" asked Jim.

"Of course... the main idea expressed here is life, not death, which is why blood, of the grape or of an animate being, is... such... an important... factor." Paul breathed in heavily, and out even more heavily. "In the same way that virginity is no longer corporately prized as something sacred by our nation, so marriage... is no longer corporately prized as sacred either... neither is even deemed useful, corporately. Covenants... are no longer understood by modern, western civilization. Instead, marriage... has been reduced to a mere contract... a legality, and the loss of virginity... is even *celebrated* outside the context of marriage! Just flip on a screen! The union is viewed as amusement.... What soul whose chief aim in life is to entertain himself... to amuse himself is not a complete narcissist?

"The antithesis of Eden's design is the general consensus of our day and in our country; as such, we observe houses... falling and families being broken repeatedly. Such a catastrophe happened in the ancient east as well, and the remedy for treading upon the threshold was that the altar — that is the threshold — had to be revivified."

"'Revivified'?" asked Sarah; "You mean, covered in blood or filled with blood?" The storm raged, and Jim continually glanced back and forth at Paul and at the storm.

"Yes; covered in life to cover over death; 'to atone' means 'to cover over' in Hebrew. Since blood... was understood as vivification, invigoration, and life itself, blood then was necessary to revive... the entrance to the house; blood was necessary to rekindle the romance; but the romance that was intended in Eden was a covenantal one, not a mere contractual one." Paul's breath became more belabored. His eyes appeared to sink farther behind the dark circles that surrounded them, but he continued to say, "The intended romance... was meant to endure for life. Covenants were understood to endure for life, whereas mere contracts often carry with them a component of time that can terminate while the two contracting parties still live. Covenants were often understood as binding... until death; however, a simple contract only endures so long as the agreed-upon service is rendered." Paul looked at the young couple with pity, though they received his softening gaze as but a component of his gentle demeanor. "Would you two like some more juice or water or something?"

Sarah's eyes widened. "Sure, I'll take some more, if you don't mind," she added, having caught herself. "May I please get it? Why don't you relax a little, Paul; we've had a long walk."

With surprising sharpness, Paul replied, "No. I will serve you... and for you, Jim?"

Jim turned his attention from the storm in response to Paul; "OK... yeah, I'll have some more; thanks."

Thunder boomed repeatedly with a sound of warlike bombardment. The rain fell so heavily that it gave the appearance of drapes flapping in the wind. Paul rose with difficulty from his seat, sauntered over to the sink, pulled out the large cup from which Jim and Sarah had formerly drunk, and he began to pour in an effort to reconcile that which was once excitedly nubile. The lightning dealt the death-stroke to the nubilous expanse.

CHAPTER 45

The thunder intensified in the mid-day darkness. Each lick of lightning lit the terraced land's crimson clusters with brief moments of brilliant colors and eerie, empurpled shading. The dull browns of death's season appeared electrified with the lightning's flickers. With each heavenly flare, the dimming grounds transformed into glowing splashes outlined by stark, splitting shadows.

Paul gulped down half-of-a-cup of juice, walked back from the sink area, closed the door to the shed, and handed Sarah the large challis that she had shared with Jim outside of the shed. Paul sat down again with his cup. Jim and Sarah sat with their large, communal cup. Paul spoke again with a continually decreasing voice: "Since blood expressed life, and since covenants were life-long, it therefore stands to reason that the life-long covenant required blood; however, the original design... the original design..." Paul inhaled heavily, "...did not involve the destruction of life to acquire blood; instead, blood was utilized in the *construction* of life, the 'building' of a house, the 'building' of a family.... The threshold was as a basin, literally, and a cup is a basin." The lightning was incessant, and it served sufficiently to illumine the room.

"The covenanting parties... the man and the woman... shared the 'blood' of the grape. Also, when their marriage was consummated, under the proper circumstances, the male's vine was covered in the female's life; the mingling of the two formerly distinct natures was... enacted in order to produce a new nature; the reflection of this new nature was understood to rest upon... to rest upon... their combined image... their child... the 'fruit of the womb.'"

"So the Eden story is a love story?" asked Sarah.

"Yes, my dear!" said Paul vigorously and with an increased voice. "Yes! — and now you can understand part of the many reasons that the enemy in the story is referred to as the 'nahash,' the 'serpent,' for a synonym of the Hebrew word '*serpent*' used in the Eden narrative is '*pe'ten,*' and a word for 'threshold' is derived from the same root as the word '*pe'ten,' or 'serpent.*' Sin is constantly likened to whoredom in the Scriptures, which is a reason why pardoned humanity, His Bride, His Body, will enjoy the marriage supper of the Lamb, as it is recorded in the Book of the Unveiling, the Revelation, the Wedding. In other words, the 'serpent,' ironically, trod upon God's threshold, God's institution of life that is illustrated by the marriage covenant; so, in perfectly just punishment, the 'serpent' was trodden upon for his deceitful deeds, and he will be crushed forever. Interestingly enough, the Hebrew word for 'lamb' and a word that means 'to tread under foot' were, originally, spelled almost identically."

"So tell me again why people were killing animals on this 'sacred' threshold if the whole thing was supposed to be one, big story about love?" asked Jim.

"A Hebrew penned that 'sin, when it is fully conceived, gives birth to death.' In a manner of speaking, treading upon a threshold was… equivalent to treading upon life, specifically *newborn* life. Death was used to extinguish life, for the devil… is said to be 'the one who has the power of death' in the second… chapter of the Book of Hebrews. Since God is perfectly just, and since… sin 'gives birth to death,' you… can see why death… was the vehicle God used to tread upon sin… and this is a reason why blood… or 'life' was continually… utilized… to paint… the threshold that was to be passed over… and not tread upon. The fruit… be fruitful… be…" Paul's eyes took on the deep tinctures of the storm-clouds; he gasped, "The cluster becomes regal in the time of death! Children… I need… to close… my eyes… for a little… I'm not feeling… well… I… think… I… Jonathan, they understand! …I have kept my word to you, brother."

Paul slumped to one side and dropped his half-filled cup onto the floor.

The lighting burst forth and whipped an instant's light upon Paul's unconscious frame. The thunder clapped, and the rain fell through the wind in a manner that resembled the subtle flaps of a recently drawn stage-curtain.

CHAPTER 46

The lightning died down momentarily. The shed was completely dark.

"Paul?" said Sarah to the blackness. "Paul? Paul!" Sarah's eyes widened. Jim sat up.

"Paul!" yelled Jim as his eyes darted back and forth in an attempt to find his wife and his host.

"Jim? What happened? He's not responding!" Jim stood up instantly and slid his hand up and down the walls in search for a light-switch. "I don't think there's electricity in here; open the door!" Jim hurried to the door and flung it open as lightning sliced through the sky.

"Sarah, we have to —"

The thunder exploded.

"— get Paul home," Jim continued.

"Call someone, now!" Jim reached into his pocket, drew out his phone, and dialed in vain. Sarah leaned over Paul and put her ear to his mouth.

"There's no signal way out here; we're gonna have to carry him back to his house."

Sarah looked at Jim with a mixture of shock and dread. "You mean, through this storm? Look at it!"

"Well what else are we going to do? Is he still breathing?"

"Yes."

"We can't just leave him here like this! I'm not a doctor! You're not a doctor! What else can we do?" said Jim with agitation. Sarah began to lose her composure.

"I don't know! I don't know...."

"We can't just sit here and wait for him to wake up; he's obviously not just sleeping! We have to get help, now!" Jim looked outside at the tempest, and then back at his wife. "I'll put him on my shoulder, but you're gonna have to help me; we're a long way from his house."

"Look at it outside! We can't carry him through that! That's awful!"

"Fine! I'll go myself! We have to do something, now!"; with that, Jim darted out of the shed and onto the slick lawns. The heavy rain felt like thousands of marbles pelting him mercilessly. The entire lawn he ran upon lit up with a tremendous flash and an almost immediate roar of wrenching thunder. Jim hurried towards the direction from which they had first walked, until he heard a piercing scream.

"He's not breathing! He's not breathing!"

Jim attempted to turn around, but he slipped on the wet grass and fell with a muddy thud like thousands of grapes falling in unison. Still in motion, Jim's legs kicked as he clawed the ground in the opposite direction he had been running until he was able to reestablish the ground beneath his feet. He ran back into the shed in his mud-covered suit. Sarah held Paul in her arms. Paul's head slumped backward unnaturally.

"I don't' think he's breathing! Jim! I —" Jim ran towards Sarah and Paul and put his ear to Paul's mouth, then to his chest, then back to his mouth. Jim opened one of Paul's eyes and beheld lightning flashing off of it. Jim recoiled, but then he regained his composure and put his ear to Paul's nose.

"He's still breathing — barely. Sarah, we gotta do this thing, together! We can't wait any longer! Jim stood upright, stripped himself of his suit jacket, leaned his shoulder into Paul's waist, and with a display of strength that surprised Sarah, he hoisted Paul onto his back. "Throw my coat over his head so he stays dry," Jim barked; Sarah covered Paul as best she could. "C'mon! Let's go!" boomed Jim.

Jim passed through the recently opened doorway and stood under the awning. Sarah stood behind him. The storm's surging vehemence gave no indications that it would abate any time soon. Jim ducked his chin, stepped out into the tumult, and began trudging, as quickly as he could, through the saturated lawns, with his wife at his side.

CHAPTER 47

The storm was almost deafening. Jim and Sarah made their way through the adversity for over half of a mile. A bolt of lightning struck the top of a tree about one-hundred feet from Jim, Sarah, and Paul. As the thunder ensued, Sarah turned to see the tree fall onto the ground in a smoky ark. The multitudinous vineyard wept bloody tears as innumerable nodes birthed untimely, fallen fruit at the merciless attack of the tempest. Jim marched straight ahead undauntedly. Paul had led the two far out into his property, and the walk back to Paul's house was becoming increasingly difficult for Jim as he carried Paul on his shoulders in the midst of the downpour. Jim slipped, and he fell under the weight of Paul. In mid-fall, Jim turned his back to the ground, so that he might support Paul with his hands and chest; he caught Paul just in time as he himself was sandwiched between the mud and Paul's motionless frame.

Sarah screeched as she rapidly stooped to help the two men.

"I'm sorry, but he's getting heavy," gasped Jim regretfully. Jim rolled out from beneath Paul.

Both Jim and Sarah were covered in mud. Jim erected himself quickly and slung Paul's arm over his shoulder while Sarah arranged Jim's ruined suit-coat like a hood for Paul, who was still unconscious. Jim began to walk forward as Paul's feet dragged in the mud. Without speaking, Sarah wiggled herself under Paul's other arm, as she helped Jim carry their host. She did not realize that Jim's left ankle was sprained from his twisting fall with Paul.

The statues almost seemed to come to life with each blaze of lightning, and the relentless thunder sounded like the roar of a stadium's audience. The slick surface of the statues reflected the light from their contours so as to give the impression of animation. Their eyes pulsed with the heavens. The stone carvings stood like a crowd that watched and cheered on the struggling couple and their weakened friend. Jim and Sarah grappled with Paul. The lightning continued to ignite the sifting, smoke-colored sky like the slashes of enormous blades clashing in some fiery, celestial sword-fight.

"I love you, Sarah," Jim yelled through the storm's clamor.

"What?" shouted Sarah.

"I love you!" Jim repeated. "I didn't do it."

"What?" The storm rang loudly in the ears of the two. "You didn't do what?"

"I didn't cheat on you. I love you. I didn't cheat," panted Jim, as it was evident that he was growing tired from having carried Paul for so long a distance with an injured ankle.

"I love you too, Jim," said Sarah, as she beheld her beloved, drenched in rainwater and mud. Swirling steam rose from the top of Jim's head as his hot sweat met the cold air. Jim's ankle gave way, but Sarah caught Paul as she slumped beneath him. Jim sunk down slowly on one knee.

"Jim! Are you OK?"

"I'm fine!" yelled Jim through the blasting storm. He stood up as quickly as he could and lifted Paul from Sarah's grasp. Jim's jacket, which Sarah had draped over Paul's head to serve as a make-shift hood, fell to the ground. Jim and Sarah beheld Paul; his wet face was empty, his eyes were half-opened and blank, his jaw was slack, and the two realized that they had been struggling only with Paul's body.

Paul Gephen was no longer a denizen of Earth and its travail.

CHAPTER 48

Jim and Sarah opened Paul's back-porch door. The two entered the house, sopping, muddy, and exhausted. They laid Paul's body on his weathered couch.

"I'll get something to cover him," said Sarah. Jim winced in pain, since his ankle had swollen to twice its normal size. Jim sat down, heavily. Sarah ran down the hallway and returned almost instantly with the blanket that she had stripped off of the bed that she had slept on the previous night. Delicately, gracefully, and quietly, Sarah draped the blanket over the corpse of her grandfather's best friend, the body of the man who had wedded her to her husband, the frame of the man who taught her the origins of marriage itself. Jim's face was covered with sweat and rain that concealed his tears as he gazed up at the ceiling.

□□□

Sarah and Jim sat on the musty couch, exhausted, and frozen with a mixture of shock and grief. Sarah's head rested against Jim's shoulder. Jim sat quietly as the police helped the coroner and his men with the stretcher that supported Paul's body. Jim and Sarah saw the stretcher wheeled past the Purple Heart medal that hung on the wall, and out of Paul's front door. The young couple answered all of the necessary questions and, eventually, they left Paul's house along with the police.

☐☐☐

The drive home was quiet. Jim sat with the passenger seat reclined all the way. Sarah drove as silent tears slowly streamed down her cheeks. Though the rain had stopped, the world before her windshield appeared wet, motionless, painful, and drab; but, her husband was next to her, asleep... faithfully asleep.

CHAPTER 49

"C'mon in, Jimmy," said Brian, as he puffed away on a large cigar. Jim limped with a cane into Brian's house. "Sit down. What's wrong with your foot?" asked Brian, as he pointed towards his living-room couch. The two sat down. Jim wore an expression that was not easily discernable to Brian. "So... what's happening? What's on your mind? Why didn't you want to go to Malik's? What happened with that Paul guy? I almost shot the nose off that lion before I left that creepy place."

"Is that why you had your right hand in your jacket?" asked Jim, as his eyes continued to widen. "What in the world were you thinking? We're in peace times, buddy!" Brian smirked as Jim spoke; Jim continued: "I just wanted to rough the guy up a little, that is, until I realized 'Paul' was a chaplain in his eighties...."

"Better safe than sorry, pal," said Brian, with a mischievous grin. "What if there were bunch of guys there? Huh? What if he had a gun (?); then what?"

"You're nuts."

"Whatever..." said Brian dismissingly, "You're just lucky I was there in case there was a *real* problem."

"Anyway… man… where do I even begin?" Jim sighed as he tipped his head back and leaned into Brian's couch. "To get back to reality, the reason I didn't want to go there is because Lisa has been pursuing me, and I'm a married man."

Brian exhaled in relief and said, "I knew something was up between you two, and I couldn't bring myself to believe that you'd cheat on Sarah. I can get pretty bold, I know, but I couldn't bring myself to ask you if you were horsing around. You've always been a true-blue kinda guy, and I just couldn't think that you'd do to Sarah what my ex-wife did to me."

"Well, I didn't, man; don't worry. What happened was… well… here's how it all goes. I know you like to hang out at Malik's; it's a neat place, and I like it too… but once Lisa started working there a couple of months ago, she started flirting with me a lot. At first, I thought it was all fun and games; you know how she is."

Brian rolled his eyes and said, "Honestly, she reminds me of Jenny…."

Jim pitied his friend, who obviously still thought about his ex-wife frequently. "Yeah, you're right. Well, I thought I was on the outs with Sarah, and I guess I just wasn't thinking too clearly. You know how it's tough to keep things straight when you're really hurting? I mean, when you're really down, almost anything can seem good in comparison to what you're struggling with."

Brian turned his head somewhat aside for a second, and then he lifted it and said, "You're preaching to the choir, buddy. It's funny how sweetness can go up in smoke." The glow of Brian's cigar intensified.

With a slight frown at his own insensitivity, Jim replied, "Sorry, Brian; you know what I mean?"

Brian perked up in his usual resilient manner and said, "Don't mention it, pal. Don't mention it. Keep going."

"The more I came into Malik's, the more Lisa kept hitting on me. She started slipping me notes here and there, but I'd usually just stuff them in my pockets and toss them in the trash as soon as I left. Each time I came into Malik's, she kept coming on stronger."

"C'mon, man! You should have just told her to back off. If you were just taking those notes and not addressing the situation head on, it's no wonder she kept at it! You gotta cut those kinds of problems off at the head; that's why we weed gardens; ya know what I'm sayin'?"

Jim gave a slight, squirmish laugh and said, "Yeah... I know that *now*. If you let stuff pile up, you get one big mess in no time. I'm a married man; I entered into a covenant with Sarah. I'm the man in the relationship. I should have just bucked up and told Lisa to back off... but I was hurting, and I thought Sarah was horsing around on me. I thought that Lisa might have been there for me when I busted Sarah. I just didn't want to close that door."

Brian raised an eyebrow. "How many sentences did you just begin with 'I,' Jim?"

"Hey, I'm the one with the literature degree."

"Since 'Hey' is more of an interjection, and since 'I'm' is a contraction, it seems like the first valid word you used to defend your poor decision was 'I' again —"

"— Get off my back," said Jim, as he laughed in slight embarrassment. "Yeah, yeah, yeah… you're right. It's easy to get self-centered, self-absorbed, selfish period, when you're insides have been kicked out. I should have just asked Sarah what was going on with the whole Paul thing, and I definitely should have put Lisa in her place."

"Well have you?"

"I haven't been back to Malik's since the last time we got together a couple of days ago. I'm not going to make a special trip there, and it's not like she's going to call my house or something."

"Did you fix everything with Sarah?"

"Yeah," said Jim with a brimming smile. "Yeah, everything's fixed. Sarah and I know that we've been faithful to each other, this whole Lisa thing is over, and I'm going to be…." Brian's phone rang. "Aren't you going to answer it?"

"I'm talking with you right now; that's what I have an answering service for. Keep going."

"I just wanted you to know that I'm not a cheat, for one; but, more so, I wanted to tell you about this Paul guy...."

"Yeah! Let's hear what all went down over there. That guy's place was sure... different."

Jim pondered momentarily. "He was a good man, Brian," said Jim, as his eyes fell into a downcast state.

"What do you mean, 'was,' Jim?" Jim sighed, pointed to his bandaged ankle, and began to unravel the brief history of his time with Paul Gephen for the remainder of the afternoon.

□□□

Brian opened his front door for Jim.

"Thanks for coming over, Jimmy-boy; that was... well... that was a pretty wild story," said Brian, as smoke poured out of his mouth with each syllable.

Jim turned towards Brian and grinned. "Oh, by the way, I'm going to be a father."

CHAPTER 50

"He died? He just died (!)?" asked Tina.

Sarah's eyes welled with tears. "He looked pretty sick when I got there, and it seemed to get worse by the hour. I kept asking him if he was OK." Sarah began to unfold her time with Paul to her best friend as the two of them ate their favorite pizza.

As Sarah drew near to the conclusion of her story, Tina wrinkled her forehead, scratched her chin, and said softly, "Perhaps that's the reason why his letters sounded so urgent." Then she spoke louder: "I wonder if he knew he wasn't long for this world. I mean, why else would he, after over two years, suddenly come into your life so quickly and so dramatically? Why else would he spend his final moments on this earth with you to help you fix your own problems? Why else would he even care?"

Sarah contemplated for a moment and replied, "Maybe you're right. Maybe he made a promise to my grampa or something... I don't know... but he sure wanted Jim and me to understand what we had gotten ourselves into; that's for sure. At the same time, he seemed like a really faithful kinda person; maybe he just really believed in what he was doing.

I don't know… He sure didn't quit on me." Sarah
sat with starry, yet sad eyes, and continued. "You
should have seen his place. Who knows what all
that man knew? His entire life seemed devoted to
the knowledge of God. He lived all by himself way
up there in those mountains. I have no idea what
all those books and globes and things were about,
but I'm kicking myself for not having talked with him
sooner. Who knows what I *could* have learned? In
fact, I'm kicking myself for not being more receptive
to my grampa's invitations to talk about all that
ancient stuff… to talk with Paul…" Sarah trailed
off remorsefully. As Tina looked at her best friend,
her eyes appeared to be painted with painstaking
contrition. "Had I just learned sooner, I'd be a lot
better off."

Tina sat silently and looked at her weary friend.
"It seems to me that you got what you needed when
you needed it most."

Sarah smiled. "Thanks for all your
encouragement."

"No; thanks for all of yours."

Sarah's eyebrows rose. "*My* encouragement? —
what do you mean?"

"All that 'covenant' stuff and 'garden' stuff'
is making me think… I don't know… making me
reconsider the whole idea of 'dating'; I think I might
be getting things backward; maybe I should just ease
up with him before I get myself into another mess."

"You mean with your boyfriend?"

"Yeah. What you described as a 'blood covenant' was just something I thought adults just kinda do when they date. I've never heard about any of this 'threshold' stuff. I didn't know that part of our lives was 'sacred.' What if I'm wrecking things for myself and for my husband? — if I ever get married."

"Yeah, I know what you mean." The two looked at each other blushingly. "I wish my dad would have just told me; I would have listened; I respected him."

The two friends sat quietly as they sipped their drinks. After several moments of silence, Tina leaned forward perplexedly and said, "For as different or foreign or whatever all this stuff you told me about is, the one thing I'm not really getting is this 'paradise' thing you brought up earlier."

Sarah's eyes flashed. "I really can't make full sense of the 'paradise' thing either, but I remember that Paul said that the word 'paradise,' at least at one time, didn't mean what we think it does... 'Paradise' didn't just mean some sort of perfect place up in the sky; he said it was a type of garden that 'the ancients' understood as a 'pleasure-ground.'"

Tina furrowed her brow again. "What's a pleasure-ground?"

"Apparently, it was kinda like a zoo and a garden put together."

"Huh?"

"Well here's what Paul told me: originally, at least in the ancient east, anyway, 'gardens' and 'paradises' were enclosures."

"You mean they had walls or something?"

"Yes; gardens and paradises had walls or hedges around them, like the rim of my flowerbox."

"So what's the difference?"

"Gardens only had plants, but paradises had plants and animals."

"Like a game-park or something? Wait, is that why Paul had all those weird lawn statues you told me about?"

"Huh; I hadn't thought about that — maybe you're right; I don't know. Anyway, originally, paradises *protected* animals; later in history, paradises became game-parks for hunters. Paul mentioned something about some guy named 'Xenophon.'"

"So, you're saying that the original design was to protect the animals, like a zoo?"

"Yeah; but not just the animals... the idea was to protect *life* — 'animate' life. Gardens were planted inside of paradises. According to Paul, the only animate life inside of gardens was that of the care-taker, you know, the gardener, or gardeners."

"So the paradise was outside of the garden, just like the animals were outside the garden that was within the paradise?"

"Yeah… I guess so; he said something about how they used to bury people in gardens. So, essentially, you could make a garden into a paradise by putting animate life into the garden."

Tina thought for a moment. "I don't get it; what does that have to do with marriage? I mean, it's interesting and all, but…."

Sarah smiled slyly. "Somehow, Paul knew that I was pregnant. Out of nowhere, he asked me if I knew that the *Song of Songs* refers to a woman in terms of a 'garden' and a 'paradise?'"

"What's the *Song of Songs*?" asked Tina.

"It's some ancient Book written by some guy called King Solomon, or something."

"So why did Paul bring up this King Solomon guy?"

Sarah continued to smile; "…because Solomon referred to a woman in terms of a 'garden' and a 'paradise.'" Tina narrowed her eyes as she moved her hair behind her ears. Then, Sarah said, "If a woman is a garden, then a *pregnant* woman is a *paradise*. A garden has no animate life except for that of the care-taker, but a paradise does have animate life. If you put animate life into a garden, it becomes a paradise. When a woman becomes pregnant, she becomes a paradise; she has animate life inside of her."

"So you're saying that you think Paul brought that 'paradise' stuff up as a way of saying that he knew you were pregnant? Is that why he was trying to keep your marriage together like he was? Wait! That means he must have heard you tell Jim that you wanted a divorce...."

Sarah pondered momentarily. "I'm not sure exactly 'why' he said or did many of the things he said or did; all I know is that I walked away from him in better shape than when I first came into his house."

"If a garden is where they buried people, but a paradise was like a pregnant woman, then...."

CHAPTER 51

Jim returned from Brian's house; Sarah had yet to return from Tina's. Jim walked from the little living-room into the kitchen as he thumbed through the stack of mail that was in his hands. He sat down at the kitchen table and began to separate the mail.

A hand-written envelope, addressed to "Mr. & Mrs. Davis," caught Jim's attention. He tore the envelope open; inside was a letter that stated when and where Paul's funeral was to be held. The letter was signed by a "Mr. Gibson," and a phone number was written beneath his signature. Jim dialed the number.

"Hello?"

"Uh, yeah… hi; is this Mr. Gibson?"

"This is he; to whom am I speaking?"

"My name is Jim Davis, and I just received a letter from you. Were you a friend of Mr. Gephen or something? How did you get my address?"

"Oh… Mr. Davis. What a pleasure it is to hear from you. Yes, I was Paul's friend for many years. He called me, quite late, several nights ago. I was surprised, since I've always known him to be an early-to-bed, early-to-rise type," said the gravelly voice on the other end of the telephone. "He spoke very cryptically… ha, ha… I guess he always did sort of speak that way…. Anyway, he told me that if anything should happen, that I should contact a 'Mr. and Mrs. Davis' at the address he gave me… well, I guess, at your address. At the time, I wasn't quite sure why he was calling me so late and why he asked me to do such a thing, but he did, so I did."

Jim's forehead wrinkled as he asked, "What night was this, Sir?"

"Oh, just several days ago… last Friday night, I believe."

Jim thought to himself for a moment: 'Paul must have called Mr. Gibson shortly after Paul directed Sarah and him to guest room for the night. He must have known that he didn't have much longer; that seemed to be the only explanation as to why Paul would make such a strange phone call so late at night. Paul must have known that he was dying since just before he began mailing letters to Sarah. Paul probably never went to sleep that night'; "That's why he was so urgent…" said Jim softly into the telephone.'

"What's that?" said the aged voice in return.

"Oh, nothing; I'm just trying to put some pieces together here."

Mr. Gibson cackled on the other end of the phone as he remarked, "I always seemed to find myself in that very position after talking with Paul.

Anyway, so you received the information regarding his funeral, correct?"

"Yes, Sir; I did."

"What a shame... Paul was no kid, but it still hurts like mad to know he's gone. Did you know him well, Mr. Davis?"

"Call me Jim."

"Ok, Jim. How long did you know my old friend, Paul?"

"Only a couple of days."

"Only a couple of days? Well, you must have been quite important to him in order for him to call me so late at night like that."

Jim thought for a moment and replied, "I wish that was true, but I think it has more to do with my wife, Sarah. Sarah's grandfather was really good friends with Mr. Gephen."

"Oh? What was your wife's maiden name?"

"Peters; Sarah Peters."

"Oh! Jonathan's granddaughter? Hah!... now I get it. Oh, Jonathan and Paul went *way* back. As a matter of fact, Jonathan knew Paul before I did. Boy, that Johnny had it rough, losing his wife, son, and daughter in law... I sure did feel bad for that boy of his, Sarah's father."

"Yeah, I understand that Sarah's mother died in childbirth, right?"

"Yes, yes. Sarah's father grew up with Paul around, since Johnny and Paul were so close. Paul talked to Johnny's son for years after the death of Sarah's mother, but Johnny just wouldn't come back."

"Come back? Come back to what?"

"To the Scriptures, the Way… he didn't handle his wife's death well. I just shake my head to think of the day he died… he couldn't have had a better example to follow than Paul's… but we all make our own beds for the big sleep."

"What do you mean, Mr. Gibson?" Jim heard an elderly female voice in the background on Mr. Gibson's end of the line.

"Jim? I hate to cut it short, but I have some business to attend to. I hope to see you at the funeral in a couple of days."

"Yes, Sir; I'll be there."

"Wonderful; it'll be good to see Sarah again… although I wish it were under better circumstances. Does she still wear pig-tails? Of course not… she probably doesn't even remember me… ha, ha… take care"; Mr. Gibson hung up. Jim shrugged and then shook his head as he himself hung up. He looked up and saw Sarah coming through the front door.

"Hi, Honey," she said sweetly; "Who were you talking to just now?" Jim stood up and embraced his wife.

□□□

Peals of sobbing thunder sifted the heavens. Jim and Sarah's ride to Paul's funeral was, at first, made difficult by the driving rain, but the condensation steadily declined until it almost stopped at the base of the mountain.

As they began their ascent, a misting sprinkled the mountain road. The two of them were silent inside of Jim's little car. Sadness was, of course, a present emotion between them, but the sadness was of an unconventional sort. Since neither of them had known Paul very well, they had no longstanding history with him over which to bewail its termination; rather, they mutually grieved a history that should have been, but never was. They lamented the loss of a man who cared for them before they even knew who he was... a man who sang his swansong in order to preserve their covenantal waltz. The sky was imbued with a blue-gray bleakness, and a gentle hush pervaded the mountain road upon which the two tacitly drove.

The misting had ceased and the mountainous fog had taken over the loftier tier upon which Jim and Sarah traveled. The wet sky took on an appearance of smoke due to the heavily clouded morning. The entire mountain seemed enshrouded.

The peculiar hush of the rainy morning penetrated the emotions of Jim and Sarah. Birds remained quiet, and the various mammals one might expect to see darting to and fro in search of sustenance disappeared under the shade cast by the weighted clouds. The mingled antitheses, of vivid colors and drab death, that so characterize the fall season, augmented the quiescent ache that had bored itself into the hollows of the couple's chests.

Jim turned onto the dirt road that led to Paul's house.

□□□

The gates hung open upon their rusty hinges. The two stone gate-keepers glistened in the morning's dampness so that they gave the appearance of silent weepers who no longer had as much reason to guard a home wherein there was no life. Jim and Sarah drove up the snaking driveway and through Paul's spacious front lawn. The lawn statues glimmered with dew as small rays of lavender caused the sculptures to glow under the shifting fog.

Jim broke the silence. "Driving through here is kind of like going through a time-machine."

"Yeah... there sure is a feeling of antiquity to it all."

Jim and Sarah reached the end of the driveway, parked next to several other vehicles, rose from their car, and ventured beneath the slithering vines of the trellis. Jim limped. When they emerged from beneath the trellis, they were met by a somber, "Hello." A silver-grey-haired gentleman, who appeared to be in his eighties, was dressed finely in a sleek, black suit with silver pinstripes. He supported himself with a chrome-plated cane as he stood at the top of the steps and between the stone guardians.

"Uh… hi," responded Jim.

"You must be 'Jim and Sarah," he said as he peered through his black sunglasses.

"Yes, we're Jim and Sarah," answered Jim.

"I'm Mr. Gibson… we spoke the other evening."

"Oh… sure; hello," Jim responded, as he and Sarah ascended the steps and as he extended his right hand while he supported himself with the cane in his left.

The two men shook hands, and Mr. Gibson said softly, "Please come in. You have a cane too, eh? Is your body getting to be as uncooperative as mine? Oh, I'm just kidding; I'm just sick of being sad; ya know? — and it's only been a few days…." Mr. Gibson turned his attention to Sarah. "What a gorgeous lady you've become!"

Sarah had no idea what to say because she had no idea who Mr. Gibson was. "Uh… thanks, I guess."

"You don't remember me, I'm sure. So, rather than make you admit to it, I was a friend of your grandfather's through Paul. I saw you as a kid a couple of times," said Mr. Gibson with a consistent chuckle and jocular expression. "Don't worry about it; I'm not offended. C'mon," said Mr. Gibson, as he gave a slight wave. He ushered the couple into the family room, but then he excused himself and headed for the washroom. Jim and Sarah were left standing in the midst of people they did not know. There were about a dozen people in their seventies and eighties; there was a perceptible familiarity amongst them that caused Jim and Sarah to notice their own distinctions from the other mourners. Some ladies, bedecked in the elegance of faded times, sat daintily upon a sofa as they sipped coffee or cream soda and discussed their favorite memories of Paul. Lush piano balladry susurrated softly from Paul's turntable until the needle butted against the end of the disc's side and the record was subsequently turned over and eventually switched.

Sarah heard one of the ladies say, "Mabel, put on that Bud Powell record over there, the 45, the one Paul used to play all the time... you know... the one with Max Roach and Curley Russell." Several men, who appeared to be the ladies' husbands, thumbed through Paul's vast library.

Jim overheard portions of complicated conversations that he did not understand. He felt, again, as if he had stepped into a different time; he whispered to his wife, "It's like we're in the past and present at the same time; ya know?"

"Yeah... I do," Sarah whispered in return. "I don't know... there's something timeless about this place. It's like we don't exactly fit in here, but, at the same time, we do. I can't put my finger on it."

Jim spied two gentlemen manipulating one of Paul's globes. "I wonder who will inherit all this stuff," Jim whispered to his wife. The air was heavy with grief, though a hopeful tinge permeated what would otherwise have been a day of complete dejection. It was as though Paul's friends were perusing his books, listening to his records, and enjoying his eclectic possessions in an effort to retrieve vestiges of his respective impacts on their lives. None of Paul's earthly possessions appeared to have been acquired by superfluous fancy. Each entity that Paul had owned during his time on the earth gave Jim and Sarah the distinct impression that there was some deeper significance than what appeared on the surface. The value of Paul's possessions did not seem to amount to much financially in comparison to the effort it required to utilize those possessions for the benefit of others. It was as if nearly everything that had been Paul's preserved some deep knowledge of some almost forgotten history that taught some timeless message.

In the midst of the page turning, the record playing, and the manipulations of terrestrial and celestial models, the various mourners all shared a variety of recollections about Paul. Two men who stood over a large globe discussed how Paul had explained something stellar to them that related to something they had been reading. The men who thumbed through Paul's books seemed to be cross-referencing tidbits of knowledge that had been shared in fractured, though fitting, form by Paul. The aroma of coffee that steamed from the mourners' cups, the hint of cigar smoke that clung to the men's old suits, and the must of aging pages all combined to elicit Sarah's memories of her grandfather. The weight of the personal relationships that appeared to bond the small band of mourners seemed impenetrable. Mr. Gibson reappeared with his stately-looking, silver-haired wife at his side. "I would like you two to meet Mrs. Gibson."

"Oh, you can call me Gertrude," said Mrs. Gibson. I understand that you two were with Paul when he passed." Jim and Sarah's countenances fell as if they had been afflicted with an invisible wound that cracked the glass of their previously dry eyes. Four men, in landscaping clothes, accompanied by their wives, entered the room with sweaty brows. "My husband and I," continued Gertrude, "knew Paul for over 50 years; he must have known that he wasn't long for this world, although we can't imagine that he knew he would be so close to meeting his Maker. He was always so considerate... and we can't imagine that he would have deliberately put the two of you in such a difficult position out there in that little shed of his. How horrible...."

"Ladies and gentlemen," the preacher interrupted; "it's time to begin." The preacher led the small congregation into another room, the room where Paul's open coffin was displayed.

□□□

At the conclusion of the service, the pallbearers, who were the landscapers, closed and secured the coffin, lifted it, and carried it towards the back porch. The small group followed in silence. Sniffles soughed through the speechless walk. A hearse was parked on the grass immediately before the back-porch, and it was pointed towards the open gates of Paul's garden. After having loaded the coffin into the hearse, the landscapers entered the car, and the driver slowly drove on the lawn, through open gates, turned east, and disappeared. The dispirited band of mourners followed Mr. Gibson into Paul's stone paradise.

The human and animal sculptures provoked the notice of all who trekked through the moist terrain. Gentle remarks of memorable merriment and present dreariness began to mingle with the perfumed air that smelled of incense. Death and life, fear and love, sorrow and satisfaction, present and past all swirled together in a winding maze of vegetation bedewed beneath the dampening mist and the braid of darkness and light that wove the morning to the sunset of Paul's life. After about 10 minutes of walking in a direction that Paul had not taken Jim and Sarah, Mr. Gibson said with a sigh, "Here we are."

Jim, Sarah, and the other mourners stood before another set of doors that joined another stone wall that stood behind another set of trees and bushes. There was a smaller garden within the larger paradise. Another set of stone guardians stood on either side of the locked doors. Though the locked garden before them was much smaller than the grounds they stood within, the stone guardians were the same size as those who watched the outside of the grounds, though these statues were of a different form. These statues stood upright on human feet, but they had the scales of fish, the wings of eagles, the horns of bulls, and the faces of women. The figure of a Man, on bended knee, was perched above the lintel. A sign depended from the door that read,

"SHE SMILED UPON MY HEART'S
SLATE WHERE HAPPINESS SWELLED;
BUT NOW, HER SWEET, SOFT SMILE
TO MEMORY I MELD."

The mourners filed into the previously locked domain and beheld only what Mr. Gibson and his wife had expected. A plot of earth had been opened to receive the coffin of Paul Gephen. The workers stood nearby the coffin and the grave in readiness to begin the burial process at the conclusion of the service. From the perspective of one who faced the tombstone, the opened earth lay to the left of a sweeping, regal, gorgeous statue upon an impressive pedestal. The

statue was of an entrancing lady with a perfectly
blissful countenance and exceedingly ravishing form;
however, this figure was peculiar in that her stomach
bulged with a distinct curvature.

□□□

The preacher finished speaking and pointed to
Mr. Gibson who said,

"Over 50 years ago, my wife Gertrude and I
stood next to our dear friend, Paul, in this very place.
His beloved, pregnant wife, died in a car accident
only several months after Paul was drafted. Our good
friend lost both his wife and child in a single day.

"Since most of you here knew Paul for many
years, you know that he was a man to whom all of
us owe a great debt; however, of those of us standing
here today, only my wife and I knew Paul during
his loss. Our dignified friend nearly lost his faith
at the loss of his wife, the bone of his bone and the
flesh of his flesh. However, Paul's Purple Heart beat
beyond the medal he earned in the war, for he never
fell away from his belief in God, his desire to follow
Him through the Scriptures, and his passion to help
others to do the same. I must say that it is a grievous
thing to know that, though Paul helped countless
people, only a few of us stand here today to honor
him.

"Though our good friend suffered terribly upon
the passing of his beloved and his only child, he kept

the Faith, and he made it his mission to help others. Each of us who stands here today has faced trials and has experienced triumphs, and each of us, I'm sure, will be quick to remember his or her thankfulness to Paul, who aided us all in countless ways." Mr. Gibson reached into his pants' pocket and accidentally pulled out his keys; then he pulled out a folded note from the same pocket. "Several days ago, Paul phoned me to tell me that he was mailing me a letter; he told me to read it aloud the next time I came to his house. At the time, I was ignorant of Paul's ailments, and, knowing Paul, I'm sure no one else here knew of them either.

"It is my honor to express my thankfulness to God for our departed friend, and it is my privilege to read this letter; however, since all of us who stand here are standing with our spouses, I'm not sure why Paul discussed 'divorce' in this letter. I'm sure he had his reasons; whatever they were, please allow me to read what our dear friend wrote:

> *What love is possible without the exposure of one's heart? The removal of one's side and the wound of a spear can both expose the same. Where hope and reality cross, even the most pierced heart can, with outstretched arms, cover a loved-one with purifying forgiveness in an effort to revitalize that which has become parched. The point of commencement and the point of termination are identical on a ring.*

A riddle has its author, and a maze has its maker. Is not love a labyrinthine enigma whose path can only be tread with the utmost commitment? Some lessons are best taught with riddles. When an author propounds a riddle, the only word that cannot be spoken by the author is the answer to the riddle. The word "divorce" was already used during our time together, so it cannot possibly be the answer. Seek the Name of the True Vine and the door will be opened, for both the answer to the riddle and the Author are One and the same.

CHAPTER 52

The final chapter is like the first, and the circuit has been completed. What was once a small garden is now a....

□□□

The bright, Saturday morning was crisp, dewy, and cloudless. Sunlight filled the blithe sky and the shine of the season spilled through an open window into the living-room of Jim and Sarah. Jim stood before the bathroom mirror and groomed his grin. Sarah stood in the living-room and looked through the window; then, she occupied herself with their infant son.

Jim emerged from the bathroom in his soft, azure robe and new, forest-green slippers. Sarah stood with her back to him as she busied herself with the delicate bundle in her arms. Sarah's sweet humming tickled Jim's ears. Jim's aftershave produced a fresh, stately scent that caught Sarah's attention, and she turned with a radiant, widening smile towards her husband as she cradled their joy in her arms. Jim smiled in return, walked past a globe, and approached his beautiful wife. The two stood silently with their infant son in Sarah's hands between them.

Jim leaned over and stroked his son's hair; he then gazed into the windows of Sarah's felicity and gave her an affectionate, little peck upon her forehead. She looked up at Jim with an even greater gleam than when she had first held her flower-box garden. With a smile that reflected the fruit of a paradise, Sarah raised their child a couple of inches and asked, "What do you think?"

EPILOGUE

The manuscript for this book was originally completed in 2009; however, for various reasons, it did not go to press until 2011. It causes me to raise an eyebrow when I consider the fact that this project began with Miss Rehanek's agreement to be my editor, and it ended with Miss Rehanek's consent to become Mrs. Collins.

THE THRESHOLD OF PARADISE

A NOVEL

BY JOSHUA COLLINS

ISBN 978-1-935434-59-7